Nils Hasler

Modelling Human Pose and Shape Based on a Database of Human 3D Scans

Nils Hasler

Modelling Human Pose and Shape Based on a Database of Human 3D Scans

Model Generation and Shape Morphing

Südwestdeutscher Verlag für Hochschulschriften

Impressum / Imprint
Bibliografische Information der Deutschen Nationalbibliothek: Die Deutsche Nationalbibliothek verzeichnet diese Publikation in der Deutschen Nationalbibliografie; detaillierte bibliografische Daten sind im Internet über http://dnb.d-nb.de abrufbar.
Alle in diesem Buch genannten Marken und Produktnamen unterliegen warenzeichen-, marken- oder patentrechtlichem Schutz bzw. sind Warenzeichen oder eingetragene Warenzeichen der jeweiligen Inhaber. Die Wiedergabe von Marken, Produktnamen, Gebrauchsnamen, Handelsnamen, Warenbezeichnungen u.s.w. in diesem Werk berechtigt auch ohne besondere Kennzeichnung nicht zu der Annahme, dass solche Namen im Sinne der Warenzeichen- und Markenschutzgesetzgebung als frei zu betrachten wären und daher von jedermann benutzt werden dürften.

Bibliographic information published by the Deutsche Nationalbibliothek: The Deutsche Nationalbibliothek lists this publication in the Deutsche Nationalbibliografie; detailed bibliographic data are available in the Internet at http://dnb.d-nb.de.
Any brand names and product names mentioned in this book are subject to trademark, brand or patent protection and are trademarks or registered trademarks of their respective holders. The use of brand names, product names, common names, trade names, product descriptions etc. even without a particular marking in this work is in no way to be construed to mean that such names may be regarded as unrestricted in respect of trademark and brand protection legislation and could thus be used by anyone.

Verlag / Publisher:
Südwestdeutscher Verlag für Hochschulschriften
ist ein Imprint der / is a trademark of
OmniScriptum GmbH & Co. KG
Heinrich-Böcking-Str. 6-8, 66121 Saarbrücken, Deutschland / Germany
Email: info@svh-verlag.de

Herstellung: siehe letzte Seite /
Printed at: see last page
ISBN: 978-3-8381-2329-5

Zugl. / Approved by: Saarbrücken, Saarland University, Dissertation, 2010

Copyright © 2011 OmniScriptum GmbH & Co. KG
Alle Rechte vorbehalten. / All rights reserved. Saarbrücken 2011

Abstract

Generating realistic human shapes and motion is an important task both in the motion picture industry and in computer games. In feature films, high quality and believability are the most important characteristics. Additionally, when creating virtual doubles the generated charactes have to match as closely as possible to given real persons. In contrast, in computer games the level of realism does not need to be as high but real-time performance is essential. It is desirable to meet all these requirements with a general model of human pose and shape.

In addition, many markerless human tracking methods applied, *e.g.*, in biomedicine or sports science can benefit greatly from the availability of such a model because most methods require a 3D model of the tracked subject as input, which can be generated on-the-fly given a suitable shape and pose model.

In this thesis, a comprehensive procedure is presented to generate different general models of human pose. A database of 3D scans spanning the space of human pose and shape variations is introduced. Then, four different approaches for transforming the database into a general model of human pose and shape are presented, which improve the current state of the art. Experiments are performed to evaluate and compare the proposed models on real-world problems, *i.e.*, characters are generated given semantic constraints and the underlying shape and pose of humans given 3D scans, multi-view video, or uncalibrated monocular images is estimated.

Kurzfassung

Die Erzeugung realistischer Menschenmodelle ist eine wichtige Anwendung in der Filmindustrie und bei Computerspielen. In Spielen ist Echtzeitsynthese unabdingbar aber der Detailgrad muß nicht so hoch sein wie in Filmen. Für virtuelle Doubles, wie sie z.B. in Filmen eingesetzt werden, muss der generierte Charakter dem gegebenen realen Menschen möglichst ähnlich sein. Mit einem generellen Modell für menschliche Pose und Körperform ist es möglich alle diese Anforderungen zu erfüllen.

Zusätzlich können viele Verfahren zur markerlosen Bewegungserfassung, wie sie z.B. in der Biomedizin oder in den Sportwissenschaften eingesetzt werden, von einem generellen Modell für Pose und Körperform profitieren. Da diese ein 3D Modell der erfassten Person benötigen, das jetzt zur Laufzeit generiert werden kann.

In dieser Doktorarbeit wird ein umfassender Ansatz vorgestellt, um verschiedene Modelle für Pose und Körperform zu berechnen. Zunächst wird eine Datenbank von 3D Scans aufgebaut, die Pose- und Körperformvariationen von Menschen umfasst. Dann werden vier verschiedene Verfahren eingeführt, die daraus generelle Modelle für Pose und Körperform berechnen und Probleme beim Stand der Technik beheben. Die vorgestellten Modelle werden auf realistischen Problemstellungen getestet. So werden Menschenmodelle aus einigen wenigen Randbedingungen erzeugt und Pose und Körperform von Probanden wird aus 3D Scans, Multi-Kamera Videodaten und Einzelbildern der bekleideten Personen geschätzt.

Acknowledgements

It is a pleasure to thank the many people who made this thesis possible.

I would like to express my deep gratitude to my supervisor, Prof. Dr. Hans-Peter Seidel for providing the inspiring, liberal environment the MPI Informatik in general and the Computer Graphics Group in particular has been for me.

It is difficult to overstate my gratitude to my direct supervisors, Prof. Dr.-Ing. Bodo Rosenhahn and Dr.-Ing. Thorsten Thormählen. Throughout my thesis-writing period, first Bodo and later also Thorsten tirelessly provided me with incitement, impulse, feedback, fortitude, and intimate fellowship. Overall, with curiously orthogonal approaches they taught me to stand my scientific ground.

I am indebted to my many colleagues for creating the stimulating, challenging, fun, and cooperative environment that predominated the time I spent at the MPII. In particular, I owe my deepest gratitude to Dr.-Ing. Carsten Stoll for long hours of fruitful discussion and well-nigh parental guidance in all matters of geometry processing. Similarly, Dr. Hanno Ackermann lovingly introduced me to the Art and Zen of Matrix Factorisation.

I would like to thank Andreas Baak and Dr. Matthias Seeger for taking me rock climbing in the hour of dire need and I am grateful to the Malteser Hilfsdienst Saarbrücken where I got to know and love a community of professional, but contagiously collegial characters.

Without the loving support my parents and brothers bestowed on me, I would not be here.

thanks for making a simple thesis very happy

Contents

1	**Introduction**	**1**
	1.1 Overview	3
	1.2 Contributions	7
	1.3 List of Publications	8
	1.4 Additional Publications	8
2	**Related Work**	**11**
	2.1 3D Acquisition	11
	2.2 3D Object Representations	15
	2.3 Shape Editing	20
	2.4 Modelling Human Shape	25
	2.5 Pose Estimation and Motion Capture	28
3	**Scan Database & Registration**	**33**
	3.1 Scan Database	34
	3.2 Registration	35
	3.3 Skeleton Based Pose Estimation	38
	3.4 Non-Rigid Registration	38
	3.5 Discussion	40
4	**Model Representations**	**43**
	4.1 Rotational Invariance	43
	4.2 Splitting Shape and Pose	48
	4.3 Factorisation	50
	4.4 Skeleton Based Description	53
	4.5 Discussion	66

5	**Generative Applications**	**71**
	5.1 Morphing	72
	5.2 Semantic Constraints	72
	5.3 Character Generation	77
	5.4 Handle Based Body Shape Modelling	78
	5.5 Animation	80
	5.6 Real-time Animation	81
	5.7 Discussion	82
6	**Estimation Applications**	**87**
	6.1 Shape Estimation from Dressed 3D Scans	88
	6.2 Pose and Body Shape Estimation	97
	6.3 Shape Estimation from Multi-View Images	103
	6.4 Tracking and Shape Stability	106
	6.5 Estimating Pose and Shape from Photographs	107
	6.6 Uncalibrated Monocular Pose Estimation	107
	6.7 Discussion	114
7	**Conclusion and Future Work**	**117**
	Bibliography	**121**

to Emmy

> Desine-moi un mouton!
>
> *Le Petit Prince*
> Antoine de Saint-Exupéry

Chapter 1

Introduction

Creating models of humans is an important task in many fields related to computer graphics. Most notably, in video games and modern movie productions a large number of synthetic characters are employed.

The requirements for these models are diverse. For virtual doubles, as used, *e.g.*, in action oriented movie productions, the created model should closely resemble existing persons. Additionally, high quality requirements are very common in motion picture productions. On the other hand, real-time performance is not necessary, since special effects for motion pictures are rendered offline on large server farms.

In other applications in the movie or game industry it may be necessary to generate and animate dozens to thousands of human characters, for example when simulating a crowded street or a virtual battle field. Here, the quality requirements are less stringent, since a large number of characters are displayed and the individual character is featured less prominently. Instead, high performance is required, as many characters need to be animated and displayed simultaneously.

Computer games have strict real-time requirements but the visual quality does not need to be as high. Additionally, as a result of the frequently restricted scenarios games are commonly set in, approaches for generating humans can often be tailored to the specific application.

In contrast, vision applications sometimes have lower quality requirements in terms of fine details of the mesh surface. Yet, it is important that the analysis-by-synthesis optimisation algorithms employed to estimate shape and pose are able to explore the solution space freely but are still constrained to realistic solutions.

Two approaches for creating required human 3D models are traditionally available. Models can either be created by hand or by using 3D acquisition systems. Modelling by hand involves significant amounts of manual labour. Despite this drawback, it is the standard approach used today, both in high-quality productions, *e.g.*, for motion pictures, as well as for comparably low quality applications in games. The main advantage of the manual approach is, that it allows for full artistic control of the result. Unrealistic body proportions can be modelled just as easily as realistic humans.

When a 3D scanner or similar device is used, only models of real, existing humans can be created. The main advantage is that the acquisition procedure is very fast and the attainable level of detail is high. It is still necessary to perform some post-processing, in order to create an animatable model. For example, a skeleton has to be fitted into the mesh and skinning weights must be assigned to the surface vertices. This can either be done manually, by a rigging artist, or an automatic approach, such as [8], can be used.

For some problems neither approach is practical. When creating a virtual crowd with thousands of characters, where each individual person is required to look different, it is impossible to manually model or scan such a large number of humans. One solution to this problem is to create a parametric model describing admissible shape variations. Several procedures for creating such a model exist. It can be created by manually modelling a number of humans and deformation fields for morphing a base character. This path is, for example, taken by the

MakeHuman project [63]. Similar approaches are also used to allow the player of a video game to customise his/her avatar. However, just like the manual modelling of individual characters, the invested amount of work is significant.

Another approach is to learn the model from a database of 3D scans. Achieving a high expressiveness is only possible if a very diverse database is available. An advantage of the method is that a strong prior towards realistic human shapes is available, since the model is based on real data.

A small number of works have been published that use this approach. Most prominently, Blanz and Vetter [10] create a shape model of faces. Allen *et al.* [3] and Seo and Magnenat-Thalmann [93] train a shape model given a set of 3D scans of humans captured in an upright standing pose. Animation of the pose is performed by embedding a skeleton into the mesh. These approaches cannot be applied directly to pose modelling because the strong articulation of humans introduces non-linearities that cannot be represented easily. Anguelov *et al.* [6] propose to also learn the pose deformation from a set of 3D scans of one subject in different poses. They are able to model muscle bulging but since only one subject is captured in more than one pose, no general correlations between pose and shape can be learned.

In this thesis, different methods for computing shape models based on a large database of 3D scans including many subjects each scanned in a number of different poses are introduced, evaluated, and compared. Additionally, several vision applications based on the suggested methods are introduced.

1.1 Overview

Starting from a database of 3D scans, the aim of this thesis is to create a statistical model of human pose and body shape. The overall approach is summarised in Figure 1.1. First, *3D scanning* and *non-rigid registration* are performed to acquire a database of 3D meshes that are in semantic correspondence. Then,

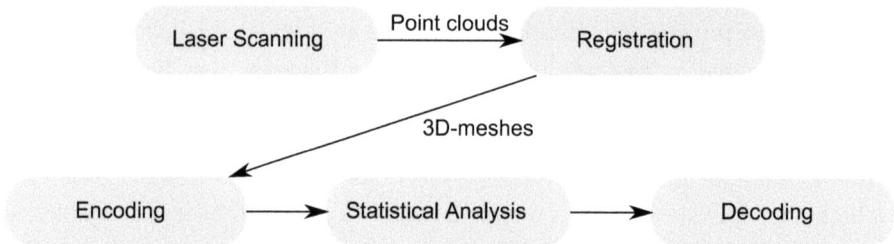

FIGURE 1.1: This figure shows the general pipeline used in this thesis to create the human shape models. Laser scanning transforms real humans into 3D point clouds. Registration achieves two objectives. Semantic correspondences between the different scans are established and the point clouds are transformed into watertight triangle meshes with identical connectivity. Encoding and decoding are inverse, non-linear transformations projecting the meshes into a space that simplifies statistical analysis and back.

before performing *statistical analysis*, the meshes are encoded non-linearly. This is necessary, because the deformation that highly articulated models such as humans undergo during pose conformation is extremely non-linear when observed in 3D space. Four different encodings are introduced that reversibly encode the 3D meshes such that the most common pose and shape variations can be approximated linearly. Linear principal component analysis can then be used to extract the main modes of variation present in the database.

Details about the database of 3D scans of human subjects are presented in Section 3.1. The design goal of the database is to span the joined space of human shapes and poses. Covering the space of shapes is achieved by scanning a large number of different human subjects. Each subject is captured in a random subset of a set of poses, which has been designed specifically to sample the space human articulation spans. This procedure ensures that the human articulation space is covered sufficiently densely to allow the trained models to generalise well.

As a preprocessing step, it is necessary to establish correspondences between the 3D scans. Without establishing semantic correspondences between the input

1.1. Overview

meshes, no meaningful statistical analysis can be performed. Non-rigid registration is performed to instantiate semantic correspondences, *i.e.*, an ICP based non-rigid registration procedure is used to fit a manually designed template 3D mesh to every scan (*cf*. Section 3.2).

Four different representations targeted at different application fields are introduced in Chapter 4. The model representations are ordered by quality of the synthesised 3D models and, at the same time, inversely in speed of synthesis.

The highest quality representation is based on the observation that an efficient encoding for a model of human pose and shape can be found if rigid and non-rigid deformations are identified individually. The extracted rotations of triangles are stored relative to their neighbours' rotations. This extension of differential coordinates to rotations allows the efficient joint encoding of pose and shape changes. In this representation, *e.g.*, bending the elbow results in changes of the encoding only in the elbow region, although position and rotation of forearm and hand change significantly. An additional advantage of the approach is that correlations between shape and pose are captured automatically. The method is described in detail in Section 4.1 [51].

One disadvantage of the encoding is that it does not allow independent control of pose and shape parameters. Yet, in some applications, *e.g.*, markerless motion capture, this is an important requirement. It allows integrating the natural constraint that the shape of a tracked subject has to remain constant and only pose is allowed to change. Two approaches for separating pose and shape contributions are introduced here. The first one is based directly on the differential rotation encoding. Only, it is assumed that an encoded 3D model can be represented as a sum of two such encodings, one pertaining only to pose changes and one describing shape variations. An approach for deriving such a split is introduced in Section 4.2.

The method presented in Section 4.3 is based on factorisation. Every triangle of a 3D model is represented as the transformation of a predetermined template model. Assuming a bilinear model of pose and shape, this transformation can be split into two consecutively applied transformations. The first one modifies shape and the second pose. Similar to the previous approach, controlling shape and pose separately is possible [48].

The focus of the fourth model (Section 4.4) is on designing a procedure for learning the parameters of a limited linear blend skinning representation to best reproduce the training data – the database of 3D scans. The current industry standard, linear blend skinning, is used because this representation is compatible with most game engines and modelling packages used today. The resulting 3D models can consequently be used readily by a wide audience for real-time synthesis of humans [52].

Chapters 5 and 6 explore possible applications of the model. Chapter 5 focuses on generative methods, *i.e.*, how to generate meshes given semantically meaningful constraints. Specifically, three methods are explored. Semantic functions are computed that allow morphing a person or generating meshes given one or more of these constraints. Then, an approach for morphing meshes using 3D marker positions as constraints is introduced in Section 5.4. Finally, the skeleton-based model, introduced in Section 4.4 can be used for real-time morphing of both shape and pose [51, 52].

In addition to animation and morphing based on semantically meaningful constraints, the most obvious applications of a pose and shape model, can be found in computer vision. Some vision tasks, explored in Chapter 6, can benefit greatly from the availability of such a model. In particular, estimating shape and pose from 3D scans (Section 6.1), calibrated multi-view images and videos (Sec. 6.3 and 6.4), and monocular images (Sec. 6.5 and 6.6) are presented [48].

1.2 Contributions

A database of 3D scans designed to span the space of human pose and shape is presented and published to the scientific public [47]. Four representations of human shape and pose, each targeted at a different field of application, are introduced:

1. A high quality model jointly describing human pose and body shape is described. The elegant encoding is automatically able to represent correlations between pose and shape but is comparably slow [51].

2. A modified version of the encoding is proposed that allows independent control of shape and pose parameters. This gain in controlability is traded for loss of correlations between shape and pose, which cannot be represented any longer.

3. A factorisation based method is proposed that is unable to capture correlations between pose and shape but is faster and more suitable for vision tasks [48].

4. A procedure for real-time synthesis of shapes and poses that is solely based on linear blend skinning skeletons is presented [52]. Unlike the other approaches, the main contribution is the procedure for generating the model rather than the representation itself.

The models are applied to variations of the human shape and pose estimation problem in computer vision. Estimation is performed, given different types of input data. Experiments are also performed with dressed subjects, introducing additional ambiguities. Three data sources are experimented with: 3D scans, calibrated multi-view video and images, and monocular images.

1.3 List of Publications

- HASLER, N., ROSENHAHN, B., AND SEIDEL, H.-P. Reverse engineering garments. In *Mirage* (Rocquencourt, France, Mar. 2007), A. Gagalowicz and W. Philips, Eds., Springer-Verlag, pp. 200–211.

- HASLER, N., STOLL, C., SUNKEL, M., ROSENHAHN, B., AND SEIDEL, H.-P. A statistical model of human pose and body shape. In *Eurographics* (Munich, Germany, Mar. 2009), P. Dutré and M. Stamminger, Eds., no. 28.

- HASLER, N., THORMÄHLEN, T., ROSENHAHN, B., AND SEIDEL, H.-P. Learning skeletons for shape and pose. In *ACM SIGGRAPH Symposium on Interactive 3D Graphics and Games (I3D 2010)* (Washington DC, USA, Feb. 2010).

- HASLER, N., ACKERMANN, H., ROSENHAHN, B., THORMÄHLEN, T., AND SEIDEL, H.-P. Multilinear pose and body shape estimation of dressed subjects from image sets. In *IEEE Conference on Computer Vision and Pattern Recognition* (2010).

1.4 Additional Publications

- HASLER, N., ASBACH, M., ROSENHAHN, B., OHM, J.-R., AND SEIDEL, H.-P. Physically based tracking of cloth. In *Proceedings of the International Workshop on Vision, Modeling and Visualization 2006* (Aachen, Germany, Nov. 2006).

- HASLER, N., ROSENHAHN, B., ASBACH, M., OHM, J.-R., AND SEIDEL, H.-P. An analysis-by-synthesis approach to tracking of textiles. In *Proceedings of the International Workshop on Motion and Video Computing* (Austin, Texas, USA, Feb. 2007).

1.4. Additional Publications

- HASLER, N., ROSENHAHN, B., AND SEIDEL, H.-P. Reverse engineering garments. In *Mirage* (Rocquencourt, France, Mar. 2007), A. Gagalowicz and W. Philips, Eds., Springer-Verlag, pp. 200–211.

- HASLER, N., AND HASLER, K.-P. Short-term tide prediction. In *Pattern Recognition, Proceedings of the 28th DAGM Symposium* (Heidelberg, Germany, Sept. 2007), F. A. Hamprecht, C. Schnörr, and B. Jähne, Eds., Springer-Verlag, pp. 375–384.

- HASLER, N., ROSENHAHN, B., THORMÄHLEN, T., WAND, M., GALL, J., AND SEIDEL, H.-P. Markerless motion capture with unsynchronized moving cameras. In *IEEE Conference on Computer Vision and Pattern Recognition* (Miami, USA, June 2009), pp. 224–231.

> Any sufficiently advanced technology is indistinguishable from magic.
>
> ARTHUR C. CLARKE

Chapter 2

Related Work

The work that is presented in this thesis is related primarily to three fields. The surface encoding we propose draws heavily on shape editing techniques. These foundations are introduced in Section 2.3. Since the main focus of this work is on modelling human shape and pose a review of models of shape and pose is given in Section 2.4. Finally, since one of the applications that can be realised is markerless motion capture a brief introduction into the field is presented in Section 2.5. Yet, since the first step in the global pipeline (*cf*. Fig. 1.1) uses laser scanning to acquire the shape of the subjects, an overview of 3D acquisition techniques is presented first.

2.1 3D Acquisition

Since estimating the 3D shape of objects is an important problem in many fields including reverse engineering [110], medicine [74], surveying [89], and biology [85], many methods for acquiring 3D geometry have been proposed.

2.1.1 Contact

Possibly the most intuitive method for digitising the 3D geometry of a real world object is to measure every significant point of the object by touching it. The surface can then be reconstructed by manual interaction. This approach is commonly used by artists [79]. The artist first creates a clay model of the 3D object and then uses a touch probe to digitise the 3D coordinates of salient points on the surface. The measurement tip of the probe is connected to a static ground plane via a chain of articulations. By measuring the angles of the joints of the arm 3D coordinates can be extracted. The full object is then modelled by hand using the acquired points to guide the process.

Alternatively, fully automatic machines, so-called coordinate measuring machines, have been introduced that sample a regular grid of points on the surface of the object [12]. These machines are available for very small volumes, e.g. for measuring cogwheels, but also to measure the shape of a complete car body. Similar to the large scale coordinate measuring machines, atomic force microscopy uses a measuring tip for sampling the surface of the measured object [9].

All of these approaches have in common that the scanned object has to be available to touch, it must not be too soft, otherwise the measuring tip may deform the object, and hard enough that it does not get damaged by the tip. Many of these systems are also not portable. So it is impossible to scan stationary objects.

2.1.2 Non-Contact

Non-contact methods, on the other hand, do not need to touch the object. This allows them to acquire the shape of objects that are inaccessible. All non-contact methods are based on some type of camera to remotely measure distances to the object. We can further categorise non-contact methods into

2.1. 3D Acquisition

active and passive approaches. Active techniques use controlled illumination to simplify the acquisition task. Passive methods, on the other hand, rely on uncontrolled ambient lighting.

2.1.2.1 Passive

The basic idea of passive 3D acquisition systems is that, given the position of two or more cameras in a common world coordinate system and the position of an object point in the image planes of both cameras, it is possible to compute the 3D position of the point in world coordinates. The effect that allows this computation is called motion parallax. Consider, for example, the configuration in Figure 2.1.2.1. Two cameras with focal points $\mathbf{o}_1$ and $\mathbf{o}_2$ observe a point $\mathbf{p}$. The projections of $\mathbf{p}$ into the image planes are denoted $\mathbf{p}_1$ and $\mathbf{p}_2$. If $\mathbf{o}_1$, $\mathbf{o}_2$, and $\mathbf{p}_1$ are known, then the epipolar line in the second image describes the points $\mathbf{p}_2$ can assume. This means that for a calibrated camera setup, efficient algorithms for 3D reconstruction, exploiting this constraint can be devised [46]. There are two main challenges when working with real images, however. When parts of the scene are occluded in one of the images, no correspondences can be established and the depth for those points cannot be determined directly. Similarly, for untextured regions image correspondences cannot be determined unambiguously. Normally, either interpolation is used or a global optimisation technique automatically establishes depth values for these regions. Additional problems can arise if the baseline is too wide, *i.e.* the origins of the cameras are too far apart because in this case the assumption that all surfaces are Lambertian is violated. An overview of dense 3D stereo reconstruction algorithms is presented by Scharstein and Szeliski [87]. According to them, most algorithms perform some or all of the following steps: matching cost computation, cost aggregation, disparity computation/optimisation, and disparity refinement.

An obvious extension to stereo reconstruction is multi-view reconstruction. *I.e.* more than two images are simultaneously taken into account. A naïve approach would compute disparities using pairwise images and merge the results. But of

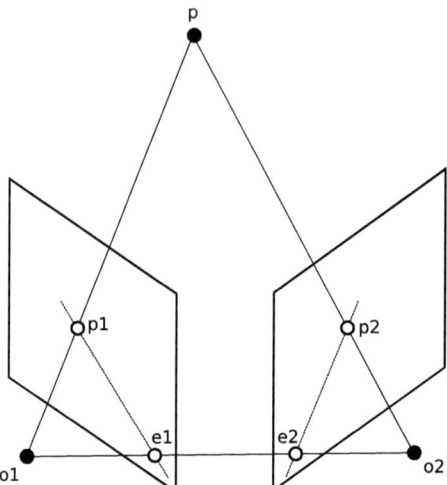

FIGURE 2.1: A point in world coordinates **p** is projected into the image plane of two cameras. These projected points are denoted $\mathbf{p_1}$ and $\mathbf{p_2}$. The focal points of the cameras $\mathbf{o_1}$ and $\mathbf{o_2}$ are also projected into the image planes. They are called epipoles $\mathbf{e_1}$ and $\mathbf{e_2}$. The dashed lines symbolise the epipolar lines.

course taking all images simultaneously into account leads to better results. An overview of multi-view stereo reconstruction techniques has been presented by Seitz et al. [92].

A further complication of the problem arises if the camera positions are not known. In this case image feature matches are used to establish both, camera parameters and sparse 3D coordinates of feature points. This is a non-linear optimisation problem frequently referred to as Structure-from-Motion [46]. Originally, these methods were targeted at video applications that involve tracking the camera position, e.g., to place virtual objects in a real scene. Yet, recently a number of papers have been presented that attempt to reconstruct the geometry of objects given an uncontrolled database of images taken at different illumination conditions by different people [42, 98].

All of the passive methods have in common that they rely on significantly textured objects to be able to establish correspondences between image features.

2.1.2.2 Active

This problem can be alleviated by projecting known patterns into the scene that selectively highlight a known ray or plane of the scene, which translates into a point or line in the image plane of a camera. Then, by using a variation of the epipolar constraint, depth can be computed. This approach is called triangulation. Alternatively, a pulse is sent and its time-of-flight until it is reflected back to the camera is measured.

The most common approaches used to acquire the 3D shape of an object employ epipolar constraints like the passive methods described above. They also use cameras but by projecting specific light patterns into the scene stronger assumptions can be made and more accurate results can be obtained. The two most common methods at the moment either project a changing pattern of parallel lines into the scene [56] or a laser sheet is swept through the scene [65]. The advantage of projecting several stripes or sinusoids in intensity space at the same time is that smaller acquisition times can be achieved but the projection necessitates the availability of a powerful high resolution and frequently also high speed projector. In comparison laser diodes for projecting sheets of light are cheap and widely available.

2.2 3D Object Representations

In order to be able to work efficiently with 3D models, it is essential that the data representations are tailored for the specific applications. In addition to the encodings introduced in this work in Chapter 4, we build on standard data representation schemes. Since, this work is only concerned with surface representation and deformation, volume representations such as voxel grids are glossed over. Here, primarily three representations are build upon. Point clouds are a very simple data structure that does not store relations between data points. The slightly more sophisticated mesh representation is able to additionally represent planar surface patches and connectivity between points. A more sophisticated representation are differential coordinates, *i.e.*, the position of points are represented relative to the position of neighbouring data points.

2.2.1 Point Clouds

As the name suggests, a point cloud $\mathcal{P}$ is a representation that stores a set (a cloud) of n points $\mathbf{p}_i$

$$\mathcal{P} = \mathbf{p}_1 \ldots \mathbf{p}_n, \quad \mathbf{p}_i \in \Re^k, \tag{2.1}$$

with k normally 3. The representation is unstructured, *i.e.*, no information about connectedness or proximity of the surface points is stored explicitly. It is easily possible to store additional information, such as a normal, colour, material properties, *etc.* along with the coordinates of the points. The main advantage of the representation is its simplicity. It is also frequently the only type of information that can be gathered with some surface acquisition systems such as laser scanners. The main disadvantage is possibly that the quality of a surface represented by a point cloud decreases rapidly with its sparsity, *i.e.* a large number of points are necessary to represent a given object well. This leads to high memory requirements and, for algorithms that scale superlinearly in n infeasible complexity. It is, however, possible to convert a point cloud into a surface mesh representation, *e.g.*, using the classical marching cubes algorithm [62].

2.2.2 Meshes

A mesh consists, like a point cloud, of a set $\mathcal{P}$ of points or, in this case, also called vertices. In addition to the vertices, however, a set $\mathcal{F}$ of m planar faces is stored. In our case, only triangular faces are considered, although higher

2.2. 3D Object Representations

flexibility is available when general polygons are considered.

$$\mathcal{F} = \mathbf{f}_1 \ldots \mathbf{f}_m, \quad \mathbf{f}_i \in \{\mathcal{P}, \mathcal{P}, \mathcal{P}\} \tag{2.2}$$

Yet, this decision not only simplifies the representation and eases local traversal of the surface but also guarantees that all faces are planar. Mesh based representations have the additional advantage that they are, especially at low resolutions, much more easily recognisable by a human than point clouds. Even for low mesh resolutions it is still possible to compute surface measures such as curvature. In contrast, point clouds are limited in this respect. Here, surface properties can only be computed if a local surface approximation is done [69]. If the surface is sampled very sparsely, large errors will be introduced using this approach because neighbourhood information cannot be estimated correctly any longer. Of course, as for point clouds, additional information can be attached to the vertices (normals, texture coordinates, colour, *etc.*) as well as to the faces.

2.2.3 Differential Coordinates

The direct benefit of switching to differential coordinates may not be as apparent as the improvement from point clouds to meshes as the stored information is the same as for meshes. However, the way it is stored, the encoding, allows some applications and processing methods that would otherwise be hard or impossible to implement.

The idea of differential coordinates is that the position of a vertex $\mathbf{p}_i$ is stored relative to the weighted sum of its one ring neighbours $\mathbf{p}_k$, *i.e.*,

$$\mathbf{p}_i = \boldsymbol{\delta}_i + \sum_k w_{ik} \mathbf{p}_k, \tag{2.3}$$

where $\boldsymbol{\delta}_i$ is the differential position of $\mathbf{p}_i$ and w_{ik} weights the sum. Formally, this representation is a discretisation of the continuous Laplace-Beltrami operator $\boldsymbol{\delta}$, as the underlying mesh can be interpreted as a piecewise linear approximation of a continuous surface [25]. In the limit case, the Laplace-Beltrami operator is the mean curvature normal of the surface, *i.e.*, the normal **n** times the mean curvature H. The same holds for the discrete Laplacian operator. As the mesh resolution approaches infinity, the discrete Laplacian approaches the mean curvature normal. In the limit $\boldsymbol{\delta}_i = H_i\mathbf{n}_i$ holds [107].

Of course, the choice of w_{ik} determines how quickly $\boldsymbol{\delta}_i$ approaches the mean curvature normal with increased mesh resolution. Many approaches for choosing w_{ik} have been presented. Alexa [1], *e.g.*, in his initial application (mesh morphing) suggested to use uniform weighting, *i.e.*, $w_{ik} = 1/b$, where b is the number of neighbours of p_i. One major advantage of this representation is that it is independent of the mesh shape - only its topology is taken into account. This approach is also called Graph Laplacian. Better results can be achieved by taking angles of the surrounding triangles into account because $\boldsymbol{\delta}_i$ converges more quickly to $H_i\mathbf{n}_i$ [15]

$$w_{ik} = \frac{1}{2}(\cot \alpha_{ik} + \cot \beta_{ik}), \qquad (2.4)$$

where α_{ik} and β_{ik} are the angles opposite to edge ik. If the tessellation is non-uniform small triangles are overemphasised. This can be compensated for by introducing a per-vertex normalisation weight $w_i = \frac{1}{A_i}$ into Equation 2.3

$$\boldsymbol{\delta}_i = w_i \sum_k w_{ik}(\mathbf{p}_k - \mathbf{p}_i). \qquad (2.5)$$

Here A_i is the Voronoi area of vertex $\mathbf{p}_i$ as proposed by Meyer *et al.* [68], using the coordinates first introduced by Pinkall and Polthier [77]. The advantage of using cotangent weights is that $\boldsymbol{\delta}_i$ contains only the normal component of the one-ring of a vertex. Otherwise, $\boldsymbol{\delta}_i$ may also contain tangential components. The cotangent weights may be negative and due to the behaviour of cot near π problematic for large angles. More well-behaved non-negative weights are the

2.2. 3D Object Representations

so-called mean value coordinates [36]

$$w_{ik} = \frac{\tan(\varphi_{ik}/2) + \tan(\theta_{ik}/2)}{\|\mathbf{p}_i - \mathbf{p}_k\|}. \tag{2.6}$$

However, the improvement in stability is only perceptible if one or more triangles are almost degenerate. Since the initial tessellation of the meshes used in this work can be controlled to be fair, no real advantage can be gained from using mean value coordinates. Especially, since in the non-degenerate case cotangent weights converge more quickly to the Laplace-Beltrami operator [15].

If a mesh is given in differential coordinates, it is possible to reconstruct the original shape by solving a linear equation system, which is built by rearranging Equation 2.3. All meshes used in this thesis are tessellated reasonably uniformly. So, Eq. (2.3) can be written as

$$\mathbf{L} \begin{pmatrix} \mathbf{p}_1 \\ \vdots \\ \mathbf{p}_n \end{pmatrix} = \boldsymbol{\delta} \tag{2.7}$$

for the whole mesh, where $\mathbf{L}$ is a sparse symmetric matrix containing the edge weights w_{ik}.

$$\mathbf{L}_{ij} = \begin{cases} -\sum_k w_{ik} & \text{for } i = j \\ w_{ij} & \text{for } j \text{ neighbour of } i \\ 0 & \text{otherwise} \end{cases} \tag{2.8}$$

Given $\mathbf{L}$ and $\boldsymbol{\delta}$ this representation uniquely describes a shape up to a global translation. This is intuitively clear because every vertex is described relative to its neighbours. Adding a global translation does not change the relative positions. Thus, the absolute coordinates of the mesh can be reconstructed (up to a global translation) by solving Equation 2.7 for $\mathbf{p}$. Algebraically speaking rank($\mathbf{L}$) = $n - k$ if $\mathbf{L}$ is an $n \times n$ matrix and the encoded object consists of k connected components [100].

As the equation system is underdetermined, additional constraints have to be added to get a unique solution. For constraining point $\mathbf{p}_i$ to lie at $\mathbf{o}_i$ set the ith column of $\mathbf{L}$ to χ_i and the corresponding row of $\boldsymbol{\delta}$ to $\chi_i \mathbf{o}_i$. Here, χ_i is a weighting factor that controls the relative importance of this particular constraint. These constraint rows can be added in two ways to the system. Either they are appended to the system, or rows are replaced. In either case, the system is quickly overdetermined. Then, both the added constraints and the shape of the object are reconstructed only approximately in the least-squares sense. However, this behaviour can be exploited to manipulate the shape. If rows are replaced these constraints are fullfiled perfectly. Added rows on the other hand are met only approximately. Notwithstanding, by changing w_i, the importance of satisfying a constraint can be adjusted.

2.3 Shape Editing

Several surveys by Sorkine [99], [100] and Botsch and Sorkine [15] have been published in the last few years shedding light onto all aspects of variational surface deformation.

Shape editing is a field in computer graphics and geometry processing that aims to develop intuitive methods for changing the shape of objects, normally meshes. The obvious application of these procedure lies in modelling but some of the methods can also be applied to shape reconstruction, tracking, and animation. In contrast to simulation, it is not necessary to produce physically correct deformations although some approaches have been derived from physically based methods [108] because behaviour that closely resembles physical performance is perceived as more intuitive. So, emphasis is put on creating intuitive and plausible deformations.

An early deformation paradigm imposes a 3D lattice onto the model that is to be deformed. The nodes of the lattice can then be moved by the user and

2.3. Shape Editing

the resulting deformation field is transferred to the model, which is transformed accordingly. Early works using this approach include [26] and [91] but even now grid based methods are still under development [14], [115].

A more intuitive paradigm has been introduced by Kobbelt *et al.* [58]. Here, handles, which can be manipulated directly by the user, and regions of influence can be defined directly on the mesh. This pattern is more intuitive to use because the deformation is performed directly on the surface, rather than indirectly, deforming a lattice, which in turn defines the deformation applied to the mesh. Often, these methods optimise energies similar to physically based deformation simulation. This approach results in a behaviour of the deformation that a user is intuitively familiar with from the real world.

Generally, all shape editing methods suffer from the inherent non-linearity of the underlying problem introduced by rotations. Consequently, many approaches have been proposed to overcome this problem. Botsch *et al.* propose to approximate a thin-plate spline energy function by embedding the mesh surface into a set of rigid prisms [13]. Non-linear optimisation leads to good deformations. Sumner *et al.* on the other hand pose the problem as non-linear interpolation/extrapolation of transformations computed for every triangle from a base pose to a set of example poses [104]. The robustness to rotations is introduced by interpolating rotations and triangle deformation independent of each other. This approach was later extended by Der *et al.* [31] who segment the mesh into parts that move approximately rigidly. Deformations are synthesised for the regions first and then extrapolated to the whole mesh. A similar idea is also used in [103]. Here, a coarse graph is overlaid on the mesh. Then, a non-linear optimisation procedure is used to compute the transformations for the graph nodes given manual constraints. An iterative Laplacian deformation method was concurrently developed by Sorkine and Alexa [101] and de Aguiar *et al.* [27]. Here, after performing a differential update step the rotation is estimated for every vertex, this rotation is performed explicitly, and the linear deformation is repeated.

A different approach is followed by Sheffer and Kraevoy [94] who define local coordinates that are invariant to rigid transformation. This is a significant step forward because it directly allows preserving local shape during editing. These pyramidal coordinates comprise edge lengths and angles between neighbouring vertices and the tangential plane of a vertex. Unfortunately, reconstructing 3D coordinates of a mesh involves solving a non-linear optimisation problem. Nonetheless, changing a 3D mesh such that significant global rotations are introduced produces convincing interpolation results.

A different set of coordinates is proposed by Kircher and Garland [57]. Their coordinates, developed in parallel with those proposed here [51], require a two-stage encoding. Differential coordinates are used to encode the shape of individual triangles and the differential transformation between neighbouring triangles is used to encode local curvature. More details are provided in Section 4.1.

2.3.1 Variational Surface Deformation

This paradigm can easily be implemented using differential coordinates. A mesh is transformed to differential coordinates and handle regions are constrained to the specified coordinates. The remaining part is then computed by reconstructing the absolute coordinates by solving the equation system.

Another interesting type of deformation is called Poisson reconstruction. This technique, which is also popular in image editing [76], can be used to join two or more objects/images such that the local gradients are preserved as closely as possible while ensuring that the two edges of the seams are co-located [116]. Botsch [16] has shown that the resulting equation systems are equivalent to the Laplacian systems described above. This can be understood intuitively by considering the following. A gradient editing operation can be thought of as changing the shape or orientation of a triangle/triangles. For example, the orientation of a body part is changed. The mesh is now partially discontinuous. However, the gradients representation can still be computed as described above

2.3. Shape Editing

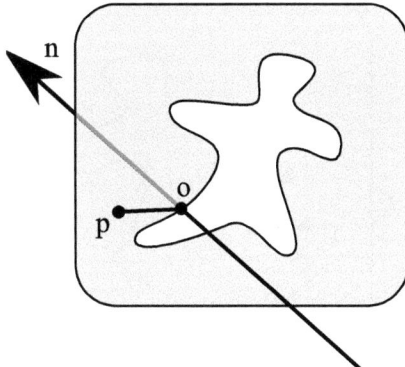

FIGURE 2.2: A point **p** is constrained to lie on the ray defined by the image space point **o** and the viewing ray **n**. This can be written as $\mathbf{N} \times (\mathbf{p} - \mathbf{o}) = 0$. This allows **p** to move freely on **n** while constraining the other two dimensions.

because the triangles (deformed or original) are still intactly representing the local gradients. Solving this system results in a closed mesh that distributes the error introduced by the rotation uniformly in the least-squares sense on the whole mesh.

For shape editing operations deformation constraints are normally set manually. In contrast, in vision applications, the constraints may be chosen automatically. In this case weighting the added equations can be used, *e.g.*, to reflect the certainty that a given constraint has been identified correctly. Additionally, in a typical vision setup, where image-based input is used to determine the deformation of a 3D shape, it is not possible to set the depth of a given constraint. Only 2D-3D constraints are available. This cannot be reflected by the constraint equations introduced above. Of course, it would be possible to make the assumption that the depth does not change significantly but this is a baseless assumption. It would be much better to constrain the vertex only in the image plane and leave the depth open for optimisation. This concept is visualised in Figure 2.2.

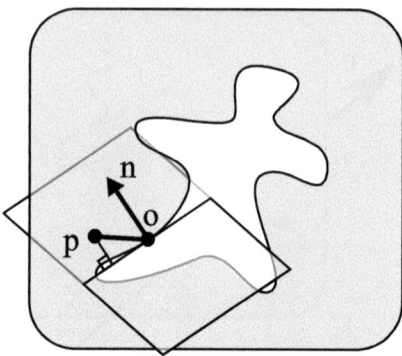

FIGURE 2.3: A point **p** is constrained to lie on a plane defined by a point **o** in the image plane and the normal **n** of the measured silhouette, **o** lies on. This allows **p** to move along the silhouette edge as well as orthogonal to the image plane.

Such a 2D-3D constraint can be represented as a cross product

$$\mathbf{n}_i \times (\mathbf{p}_i - \mathbf{o}_i) = 0. \tag{2.9}$$

Here, $\mathbf{n}_i$ is a vector in the viewing direction and $\mathbf{o}_i$ any 3D point on the viewing ray representing the image feature. Constraints of this type are frequently used in markerless motion capture [17], [20]. In a context very similar to the problem addressed in this thesis, de Aguiar et al. [29] use 2D-3D correspondences to track a deformable mesh employing a multi-camera setup. Also in the context of markerless tracking with a multi-camera setup Sunkel et al. adapt a 3D template mesh to conform more closely to the observed silhouettes [105].

There is one more type of constraint used in this work constraining a vertex in only one dimension. 1D-3D constraints are useful for matching a 3D shape to an image silhouette. Normally, when using ICP style optimisation correspondences between the projection of a 3D shape and a measured silhouette are computed. These matches define 2D-3D constraints. However, if the closest 2D point lies on an approximately straight line using 2D-3D constraints introduces unnecessary resistance against slippage along the edge. Gelfand and Guibas [41] and Bokeloh et al. [11] observe similar properties in the context of 3D object

2.4. Modelling Human Shape

FIGURE 2.4: Muscle bulging is not only a function of the underlying skeleton but is instead closely correlated with the physique of the subject.

analysis/matching. 1D-3D constraints can be written as

$$(\mathbf{p}_i - \mathbf{o}_i) \cdot \mathbf{n}_i = 0. \tag{2.10}$$

As shown in Figure 2.3 a 3D point constrained by this equation is able to move along two dimensions without changing the error.

2.4 Modelling Human Shape

The automatic generation and animation of realistic humans is an increasingly important discipline in the computer graphics community. The applications of a system that simultaneously models pose and body shape include crowd generation for movie or game projects, creation of custom avatars for online shopping or games, or usability testing of virtual prototypes. But also other problems such as human tracking or even biometric applications can benefit from such a model.

Realistic results for human animation can be obtained by simulating the tissue deformation on top of modeled skeletal bones [33, 88]. This approach has been researched extensively but involves a lot of manual modelling since not only the surface but also the bones, muscles, and other tissues have to be designed.

Additionally, these methods tend to be computationally expensive since they involve physically based tissue simulation.

In order to reduce the required amount of manual modelling, several systems have been proposed that attempt to learn general human models from 3D scans. The first systems proposed to analyse human shape only, ignoring pose. Allen *et al.* [3] are the first to present a method for computing a statistical model describing human shape given a set of 250 3D scans of humans scanned in a similar pose. The main difficulty addressed in this work is to find a parameterisation of the incomplete 3D scans that preserves semantic correspondences. Afterwards, principal component analysis is performed on the vertex positions of the registered meshes.

Similarly, Seo and Magnenat-Thalmann [93] present a method for generating or modifying human shapes given a set of 3D scans. They also fit a template model to the scan, guided by manually placed markers. The residual error of the surface after fitting the template is stored as a displacement map. New shapes are synthesised by Gaussian Radial Basis Function interpolation given a set of body measures as input. Animation of the resulting meshes is possible because a skeleton is embedded into the template and resized along with the body shape.

Azous *et al.* propose a volumetric approach to the problem [7] by voxelising the 3D scans of 300 male subjects in the CAESAR database [80]. All subjects are standing in a similar pose. Nonetheless, the slight pose variations severely influence their statistical analysis of the data.

One of the major difficulties with most previously suggested methods like SCAPE [6] or [3, 93, 112, 113] is that they rely on different means for encoding shape and pose. Pose (and the effects thereof, *e.g.*, muscle bulging) are stored with the help of an underlying skeleton while body shape is encoded using variational methods or envelope skinning. During animation, the outcomes of the two

2.4. Modelling Human Shape

methods have to be combined in an additional step, *e.g.*, by performing Poisson reconstruction.

Allen *et al.*, on the other hand, presented a method that learns skinning weights for corrective enveloping from 3D scan data [4]. They propose to use a maximum a posteriori estimation for solving a highly non-linear function which simultaneously describes pose, skinning weights, bone parameters, and vertex positions. The authors are able to change weight or height of a character during animation and the muscle deformation looks significantly more realistic than linear blend skinning. However, since this function has a high number of degrees of freedom, the optimisation procedure is very expensive. Additionally, the number of support poses that can be computed per subject is limited by the complexity of the approach, which in turn bounds the achievable realism.

A major benefit of the shared encoding is that it is easily possible to encode correlations between pose and body shape, *e.g.*, the body surface deformation generated by the motion performed by an athletic person exhibits different properties than the same motion carried out by a person with less pronounced skeletal muscles (*cf.* Fig. 2.4).

The resulting shape coefficients and their variances are analysed using a statistical method. Similar to Blanz *et al.* [10], regression functions are trained to correlate them to semantically significant values like weight, body fat content, or pose. Allen *et al.* [3] uses a simple linear method to generate models conforming to a set of semantic constraints. Allen *et al.* do not show quantitative analysis of the accuracy of their morphing functions. In contrast Seo and Magnenat-Thalmann describe a method for generating human bodies given a number of high level semantic constraints [93] and evaluate the accuracy of linear regression based morphing functions. In Section 5.2.1 a quantitative analysis comparing linear and non-linear regression functions for various body measures is presented. Scherbaum *et al.* [90] have concluded in the context of face morphing that although non-linear regression functions are numerically more accurate, the visual difference to the linear counterpart is minimal.

2.5 Pose Estimation and Motion Capture

Motion capture plays an increasingly important role in modern media productions. Traditional marker based motion capture requires actors to wear special suits, and is commonly restricted to studio environments. Several markerless motion capture systems have been proposed [70, 71]. However, most require that, in addition to the input video, a model of the tracked person (*e.g.* a 3D scan [37], a cylinder [23], or blob [18] based model) is supplied.

2.5.1 Markerless Methods

Muybridge is commonly credited for being the first to do motion analysis. His famous experiments published in 1887 [73] comprise sequences of photographies depicting the locomotion of humans and some animals. The footage was shot using arrays of synchronised cameras.

Vision based motion capture, however, was pioneered by Hogg [55] and Rohr [81] who were both able to track a person walking parallel to the viewing plane of a single camera. By using an a priori model of the human gait they effectively reduced the problem to one dimension. Both authors used skeleton-based models of the tracked human made up of cylinders which are deformed to best fit the edges of observed person and model.

Gavrila and Davis [40] introduced an approach that matches tapered superquadrics to multi-view video frames and then employs an analysis-by-synthesis technique to match a high degrees of freedom skeleton-based model to the observed data. The similarity of model and video data is also evaluated using an edge-based metric. Tracked persons are required to wear colour coded clothing.

The approach presented by Wren *et al.* [114] employs a statistical colour-based model for segmenting foreground blobs from the background. The models are updated during tracking compensating for slow changes in the background.

2.5. Pose Estimation and Motion Capture

The model of the person, commonly consisting of several blobs with different colours, is generated automatically. As the system is based on a single camera and uses simple texture analysis algorithms significantly less information can be recovered by their approach than by modern motion capture algorithms. Yet, it has to be pointed out that they were able to perform simple gesture analysis and that the proposed system works robustly even in cluttered environments.

Only a short time later Bregler and Malik [17] introduced a new mathematical method for tracking articulate bodies. By using products of exponential maps and twist motions only a simple linear system has to be solved to update the kinematic chain. This allows more sophisticated, hierarchically organised bodies with more degrees of freedom to be tracked efficiently. While their approach models humans as a hierarchy of cylinders and spheres triangular mesh models can just as well be used. An extension to the work was published by Bregler *et al.* [18] proposing a technique that also allows the automatic extraction of the kinematic chain.

The approach based on exponential maps can be extended to include additional constraints, for example by introducing motion priors [82] or by forcing body parts to adhere to geometric constraints [83].

Most of the systems mentioned above require either manual segmentation of the images/videos into fore- and background or use background subtraction to get the segmentation. This can be avoided if an iterated pose-estimation/segmentation approach is employed [19]. The segmentation algorithm is seeded with the texture covered by the initial pose estimate and based on this segments the current image. This new segmentation is used to reestimate the pose, which is used to re-seed the segmentation algorithm. These two steps are iterated until convergence is reached.

Statistically motivated methods such as Gall *et al.* [38] or Deutscher and Reid [32] attempt to overcome the limitations of local search during motion capture by stochastically sampling the space spanned by the degrees of freedom of the skeleton.

All of the approaches above have one common limitation. They require static cameras. If, however, the procedure is coupled with a camera tracking algorithm, *e.g.*, based on structure-from-motion this limitation can be dropped. The only requirement for such a system is that sufficient structured background is available. We present such a system that is additionally able to temporally synchronise the video streams of handheld cameras [50].

2.5.2 Shape Estimation

Most markerless motion capture methods have in common that they require a model of the tracked person. In the following a few works that estimate the shape of the person along with the pose are introduced.

An early method for estimating body shape from images has been presented by Hilton *et al.* [54]. They require three predefined orthogonal views to fit a deformable template model to silhouettes.

Bălan *et al.* [22] propose a system that, in addition to the pose, estimates the body shape of a tracked person in every frame of a given sequence. This becomes possible because the tracking is based on a model (SCAPE) that is able to synthesise realistic human body models.

Similarly, Sigal *et al.* [97] estimate pose and body shape in still images by training an image descriptor on silhouettes synthesised with the SCAPE model. Given an unknown image, the approach is able to roughly estimate pose and shape of the subject. A generative stochastic optimisation method is then applied to finely fit the surface of the observed human. It is also possible to estimate simple anthropometric measures from the model. Height and arm span are extracted by bringing the model into the T-pose. Length measures can then easily be extracted in 3D. By computing the volume of the mesh and assuming

2.5. Pose Estimation and Motion Capture

that human bodies primarily consist of water, an estimate of a subject's weight is also computed.

Bălan et al. [21] approach a similar problem. They also perform pose and shape estimation from single images. However, their setup includes a light source that creates a hard shadow. During optimisation they additionally estimate the position of the light source. This allows them to use the shadow as an additional projection of the subject which stabilises monocular pose estimation significantly. A disadvantage of this approach is that its use is restricted to carefully controlled in-door environments.

A system for estimating body shapes, also based on SCAPE, that is additionally robust to clothing, given images of dressed persons, was recently presented by Bălan et al. [24]. They integrate several multi-view images of a subject to improve stability of the shape estimate. Colour-based segmentation of the scans into dressed and naked parts helps them to tune the shape fitting procedure. Optimisation is performed using the direct search simplex method. Tracking results are also shown but these are initialised using a cylinder based tracker [23] and shape estimation is performed as a fine tuning step only.

In a recent work, Guan et al. [44] estimate pose and shape from single images given only a number of manual correspondences from the image and the height of the subject. After fitting the SCAPE model to the markers, the resulting mesh is used to initialise a graph cut based segmentation algorithm [84]. In addition to the silhouette they propose to use edges to improve fitting for overlapping body parts. Shading cues restrict them to naked subjects but improve the accuracy of the estimation.

2.5.3 Performance Capture

In so-called performance capture a slightly different goal is pursued. Not just the parameters of a skeleton embedded inside a mesh are estimated but, the surface of the dressed person, including folds and wrinkles is sought-after. The general approaches are similar to those used in markerless motion capture. Only mesh deformation techniques are additionally needed to reconstruct the deforming surface.

De Aguiar *et al.* [28] use a skeleton-based tracking procedure to match the pose of a tracked person to observed silhouettes. In a second step colour consistency is used to improve the resulting surface. In a later work they forego using a skeleton [27] and instead employ a mesh-deformation based procedure operating at two resolutions.

Vlasic *et al.* [111] also use a skeleton-based model for pose estimation. They also apply a similar iterated Laplacian mesh editing procedure to improve the accuracy of the surface fit. A similar approach has also been proposed by Gall *et al.* [39] who also first fit a skeleton-based template to observed silhouettes and then deform the surface to create a more accurate fit.

Chapter 3

> In theory, there is no difference between theory and practice. But, in practice, there is.
>
> JAN VAN DE SNEPSCHEUT

Scan Database & Registration

In this chapter the database of 3D scans captured as part of this thesis is introduced and the registration procedure for establishing semantic correspondences is described. When this project was initiated no database of 3D scans of humans was freely available. Consequently, it was not directly possible to generate a statistical model that would allow implementing the applications introduced in Chapters 5 and 6. So as a first step a database was designed, captured, and registered as an additional contribution. The database is designed to sample both, the space of human shapes and the space of human poses at a density that allows generic interpolation, and generation of arbitrary humans in any realistic pose.

The largest part of this chapter (Sec. 3.2 to 3.4) is concerned with the non-rigid registration procedure that brings the 3D scans into correspondence. The main challenge addressed is that the deformations for mapping one model onto another are in some cases large. Additionally, the subsequent statistical analysis requires a highly accurate registration. If the vertices are not registered accurately enough, statistical analysis fails. Linear Laplacian deformation is consequentially not an option. Instead, an optimisation framework is used that minimises the difference between neighbouring transformation matrices from a template mesh to the 3D scan.

3.1 Scan Database

The database of dense full body 3D scans was captured using a Vitronic laser scanner. Of the 114 subjects aged 17 to 61, 59 are male and 55 female. The average age is 23.6 years with a standard deviation of 6.2 years. In addition to one standard pose that allows the creation of a shape-only model, all subjects are scanned in at least 9 poses selected randomly from a set of 34 poses, which are shown in Fig. 3.1. See Fig. 3.2 for the scan distribution. The poses were designed to elaborate all major degrees of freedom of the human skeleton. Most poses elaborate one degree of freedom only, while keeping the rest of the body in the standard pose. This choice increases the number of poses but simplifies the task of explaining the pose a subject is supposed to perform, which may sound trivial but turned out to be harder than expected. The different global orientations of the scans are a result of the limited scan volume of the scanner. Some poses had to be performed to fit diagonally into the volume. All subjects were asked to make fists during scanning because the laser scanner was unable to capture flat hands with sufficient detail for the registration to work reliably. During the experiments, we realised that a significant portion of the pose set works with the head. As head motions are comparably subtle and relatively hard to register accurately we decided, after the first four subjects, to scan at most one of the head poses. This also explains the lower density for poses 18–24 in Figure 3.2.

Unlike SCAPE [6] or more recently [4] we sample the space more densely. This allows our model to capture pose–body-shape correlations more easily. Furthermore, sex, age, and self-declared fitness level are noted. Likewise, a number of measures are captured with a commercially available impedance spectroscopy body fat scale, namely weight, body fat percentage, percentage of muscle tissue, water content, and bone weight are measured. We also use a medical grade pulse oximeter to capture the oxygenation of the subjects' hemoglobin and their pulse. The scans are arranged in a database $\mathbf{S}_{s,p}$, where s is the subject identifier and p the pose, containing the points and their respective normals as generated by the scanner. This database is available to the scientific public [47].

In order to create a unified model of all the captured data, the scans have to be brought into semantic correspondence. The simplest and most common way to achieve this is to fit a single template model to every scan (*cf*. [3, 6, 10, 93]).

The symmetric template mesh is created by triangulating a 3D scan, enforcing symmetry by hand and manually fitting a skeleton into the model. Skinning is performed using the technique by Baran and Popović [8].

3.2 Registration

Non-rigid registration of 3D models is a challenging task. Starting from a common template rather than triangulating each point cloud independently, ensures identical mesh topologies and, to a certain degree, semantic correspondences are established automatically. Additionally, due to the large number of 3D scans the procedure to register all scans from the database has to be robust and almost fully automatic since the massive number of scans does not allow tedious manual intervention to be performed on every scan. We have consequently opted for a two stage process. First, skeleton-based deformation of the template is used to estimate pose and rough size of the scanned subject. Then, a non-rigid deformation technique is employed to fit the template to the scanned point cloud. Performing these two steps is necessary and desirable since the stability of non-rigid registration increases significantly when the initial mesh configuration is close to the point cloud that is to be matched. For complex poses (*cf*. Fig. 3.3)

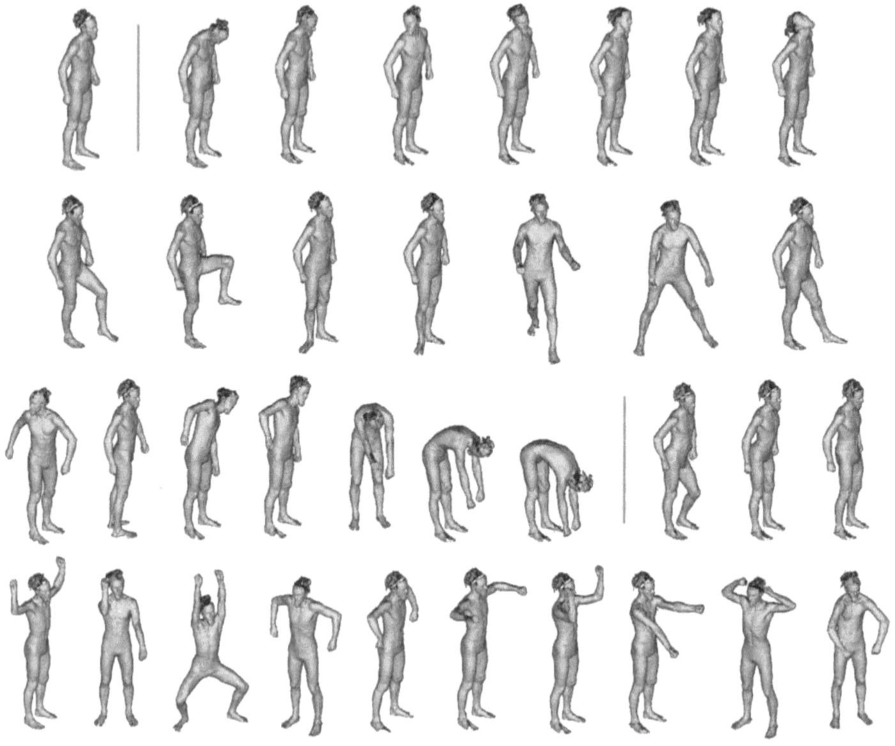

FIGURE 3.1: The poses used during scan database creation are shown. In the **top row** the standard pose, performed by every subject is shown plus the head articulations. Every subject was scanned in at most one of the head articulations. In the **second row** poses articulating hip and knee are shown. In the **third row** the three degrees of freedom of the torso and two for the hip are elaborated. The **bottom row** shows poses exploring elbow and shoulder articulations.

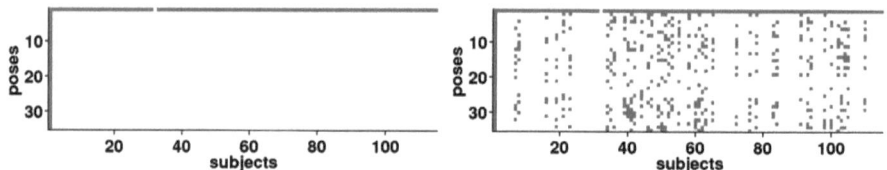

FIGURE 3.2: Every dot marks a scan taken from a subject in a given pose. **Left**: SCAPE-like approach - only one subject is scanned in different poses. **Right**: Our model covers the space of body shapes more densely.

3.2. Registration

direct non-rigid deformation converges very slowly. In contrast, due to the limited number of degrees of freedom, a skeleton based method converges quickly even in extreme cases. Using skeleton fitting for a first estimate also allows us to use the resulting data for pose regression.

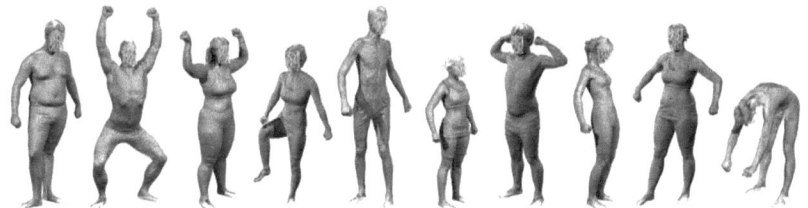

FIGURE 3.3: A few examples of scans included in our database.

The process depends only on a few manually placed correspondences for each scan as the scans do not feature any prescribed landmarks as present for example in the CAESAR database [80]. The template, an example of a labelled scan, the skeleton based fitting, and the final registration result are shown in Figure 3.4.

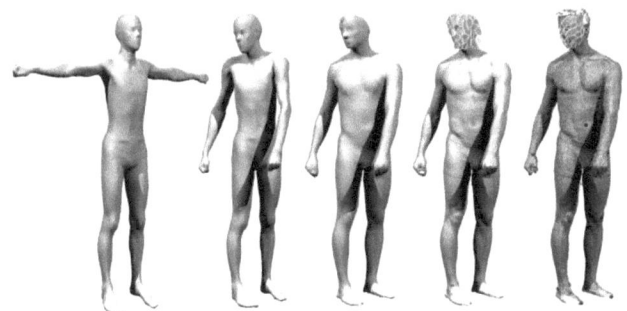

FIGURE 3.4: This figure shows the registration pipeline used in the presented approach.
Left to right: The template model, the result after pose fitting, the result after non-rigid registration, transfer of captured surface details, and the original scan annotated with manually selected landmarks are shown.

3.3 Skeleton Based Pose Estimation

The skeleton based fitting procedure employs an approach commonly used in markerless motion capture systems [17]. Any rigid body motion can be modeled as a single rotation around a chosen axis followed by a suitable translation. Together, the transformation can be stored as a twist ξ with 6 degrees of freedom. See Murray *et al.* [72] for mathematical properties and a more in depth description. The deformation of the template model is additionally governed by a kinematic chain with k joints which arises from the embedded skeleton. Only simple revolute joints are considered, which can be parameterised by a single angle γ_i. By parameterising the complete pose of a person as a vector $\Xi = [\xi, \gamma_1 \ldots \gamma_k]$ we can easily generate a linear system of constraint equations to optimise the pose. An ICP style optimisation scheme similar to Bregler *et al.* [18] is used that generates up to three constraint equations per point of the template surface. Additionally, the manually selected landmark coordinates are used to ensure global stability of the fitting process. The results from this step are used on the one hand as training data to learn regression functions for modifying the pose of a subject. On the other hand, the extracted pose can be used to initialise the non-rigid registration technique described in the following.

3.4 Non-Rigid Registration

The posed template is used as initialisation for a more detailed non-rigid registration step, that captures the remaining details of the current scan. The procedure follows the ideas presented in the work by Allen *et al.* [3] and Amberg *et al.* [5]. The registration is expressed as a set of 3×4 affine transformation matrices $\mathbf{T}_i$ associated with each vertex $\mathbf{p}_i^t$ of the posed template, which are organised in a single $4n \times 3$ matrix

$$\mathbf{X} = [\mathbf{T}_1 \ldots \mathbf{T}_n]^\top \qquad (3.1)$$

3.4. Non-Rigid Registration

We define the cost function $E(\mathbf{X})$ of our deformation as a combination of three energy terms: $E_d(\mathbf{X})$, which penalises distance between template and target surface, $E_s(\mathbf{X})$, which acts as a regularisation term to generate a smooth deformation, and finally $E_l(\mathbf{X})$, which is a simple landmark distance term,

$$E(\mathbf{X}) = \alpha E_d(\mathbf{X}) + \beta E_s(\mathbf{X}) + \gamma E_l(\mathbf{X}). \tag{3.2}$$

Unlike Amberg *et al.*, we do not express the distance term using the closest point of the target surface from the template vertices, but as a projection onto a plane fitted to a local patch of the target surface. Amberg *et al.* are forced to handle vertices bordering on holes in the target surface specially to avoid artefacts. This is not necessary if the inverse procedure is used and allows us to skip the border labelling step.

To find this projection, we first find the closest mesh vertex $\mathbf{p}_i^t$ for each target surface point $\mathbf{p}_j^s$. We discard matches where the angle between the respective normals are above a threshold $\epsilon_n = 30°$ or the distance between the points is bigger than $\epsilon_d = 50\,\mathrm{mm}$. We now go through all mesh vertices $\mathbf{p}_i^t$ and gather the set P_i of all points that were matched to it. We then use a least-squares procedure to fit a local plane to them and project the point $\mathbf{p}_i^t$ onto that plane, resulting in a target point $\tilde{\mathbf{p}}_i^t$ unless P_i contains fewer than 4 points. In the latter case the set is discarded and we assign the closest point of the surface $\mathbf{p}_j^s$ as the target position $\tilde{\mathbf{p}}_i^t$ unless this point also fails the requirements given above. Our distance energy term can now simply be expressed as

$$E_d(\mathbf{X}) = \sum \|\tilde{\mathbf{p}}_i^t - \mathbf{T}_i \mathbf{p}_i^t\|^2 \tag{3.3}$$

The regularisation term $E_s(\mathbf{X})$ in Amberg's original paper is expressed as the Frobenius-Norm of the transformation matrices of neighboring vertices in the mesh. This original term does not take into account irregular sampling of the mesh, and thus may exhibit some artifacts. Additionally, in our case missing data needs to be extrapolated only in localised regions where we have holes in the scan. In our experiments we therefore confine the second order differences of the transformation matrices by applying a Laplacian constraint with cotangent edge weights. This regularisation term tries to make changes in the transformation matrices over the mesh as smooth as possible, and not as similar as possible as originally proposed. The regularisation term can be written as

$$E_s(\mathbf{X}) = \sum \| \sum_j w_{ij}(\mathbf{T}_i - \mathbf{T}_j) \|^F \quad (3.4)$$

where w_{ij} are the cotangent Laplacian weights based on the original template mesh configuration and $\| \|^F$ denotes the Frobenius Norm.

The final term $E_l(\mathbf{X})$ is a simple landmark distance term:

$$E_l(\mathbf{X}) = \sum \| \tilde{\mathbf{l}}_i^t - \mathbf{T}_i \mathbf{p}_i^t \|^2 \quad (3.5)$$

The general registration procedure follows the work of Amberg and coworkers. The energy term (3.2) can be written as a linear system and solved in the least-squares sense for a given configuration. This process is iterated $t_{max} = 1500$ times, during which we change the energy function weighting terms in the following way:

$$\beta = k_0 \cdot e^{\lambda t}, \quad (3.6)$$

where t is the number of the iteration, $k_0 = 3000$, and

$$\lambda = \ln\left(\frac{k_0}{k_\infty}\right) / t_{max} \quad (3.7)$$

with $k_\infty = 0.01$. Additionally, α can be kept constant at 1 and $\gamma = k_\gamma \cdot \beta$ with $k_\gamma = 2$.

3.5 Discussion

In this chapter the database of 3D scans, which the rest of this thesis is based upon is introduced. It has been designed to sample the space of human shapes

3.5. Discussion

and poses at a sufficiently high sampling density such that it becomes possible to generate a model describing human shape and pose. As described in the following chapters, such a model can be used to create human shapes given semantic constraints or to regularise shape and pose estimation procedures. Obviously, the more samples are taken, the more expressive the resulting model becomes. However, a balance between quality requirements and the amount of work necessary to capture the data has to be found. After all, just capturing ten scans of one subject takes approximately 30 minutes.

The captured database is the most diverse database published to date. The CAESAR database [80] contains significantly more subjects (2400 *vs.* 114) but each subject is captured in only three poses in contrast to 10 the poses we randomly sample from a set of 35 poses. It would be possible to combine the two databases to create even more expressive models of human shape and pose. This step would significantly increase the variance of shapes as the subjects we captured are sampled from a fairly uniform population. Most of our subjects were approximately 24 year old caucasian students, whereas the CAESAR database samples a more diverse population with a higher age and ethnicity variation.

The registration procedure applied here is not the only option but experimenting with an iterated Laplacian deformation technique provided only insufficient results. More concretely, the RMSE of the fitted surfaces was good using this method but the semantic correspondence between the different scans was not preserved at an adequate level. A drawback of the current registration procedure is that it is computationally expensive. Registering a single scan takes up to an hour. As future work, an approach for iteratively improving the registration could be implemented. Using a model of human pose and shape, generated from the current scan database, the 3D scans could be fitted again. Since the model cannot represent misregistration very well because this appears as low magnitude noise after principal component analysis, refitting the scans results in a more consistent fit.

> If we knew what it was we were doing, it
> would not be called research, would it?
> ALBERT EINSTEIN

Chapter 4

Model Representations

In this chapter four different representations, describing the space of human pose and shape are introduced. In Sections 4.1 a rotation invariant encoding is presented, which allows the conjoint description of pose and shape variations. In the following section (Sec. 4.2) the encoding is modified such that pose and shape parameters can be controlled separately. A factorisation based approach is introduced in Section 4.3, which is faster to compute but is unable to capture correlations between pose and shape. Finally, a system focused on real-time synthesis of 3D models is presented in Section 4.4. It is based on the popular linear blend skinning. A learning approach to generate skeletons that represent both pose and shape variations in the same way with linear blend skinning is presented. A short discussion concludes this chapter in Section 4.5.

4.1 Rotational Invariance

It is useful to encode the registered meshes in such a way that the relevant differences between a pair of scans can be extracted easily. For example, if the subject raises an arm between two considered scans, we want the representation of the hand of the person to be identical, although both position and rotation of the hand relative to the main body have changed. Simple Laplacian coordinates cannot be used directly as they provide only translational invariance but rotational invariance is also required for highly articulated models such as humans. A common method to achieve rotational invariance is to embed a skeleton into the model and encode the surface as a function of the skeleton [6]. Additionally, the correlation between pose and body shape becomes harder to capture. *E.g.* in [6] three components are combined to create a final 3D model. The first describes shape variations, the second component encodes a kinematic skeleton and the membership of triangles to the respective bones, and the third component models non-rigid deformations as a result of the pose change. Instead of this complex approach, in the following, we describe an encoding that allows us to describe both pose and body shape in a unified way. As we show in Section 5.1, this non-linear transformation allows us to work with linear functions for modifying pose or body shape without significant loss of accuracy.

Translational invariance can easily be achieved by using variational approaches, as for example introduced by Yu *et al.* [116] or Sorkine *et al.* [102]. The mesh can be reconstructed given only the original connectivity and the triangle gradients by solving a sparse linear Poisson system. We can also edit and modify the shape by 'exploding' it, *i.e.*, applying an arbitrary transformation to each triangle separately. If we then solve the so modified linear system, we effectively stitch the triangles back together in such a way that the prescribed triangles transformations are maintained as accurately as possible in the least-squares sense. This fundamental idea has been used for shape editing (as for example in [117]), but also forms the basis of SCAPE [6].

Unfortunately, this variational representation is not invariant to rotation, meaning that the same shape will be encoded differently depending on its orientation. To remedy this, we encode each triangle as a transformation $\mathbf{U}_i$ relative to a rest-pose triangle $\mathbf{t}_i$. This transformation can be split up into a rotation $\mathbf{R}_i$ and a remaining stretching deformation $\mathbf{S}_i$ using polar-decomposition. The stretching deformation is by construction rotation-invariant, which means that we only

4.1. Rotational Invariance

need to construct a relative encoding for the rotation matrices $\mathbf{R}_i$. This can be achieved by storing relative rotations $\mathbf{R}_{i,j}$ between pairs of neighbouring triangles, *i.e.*,

$$\mathbf{R}_{i,j} = \mathbf{R}_i \cdot \mathbf{R}_j^{-1}, \tag{4.1}$$

where i and j are neighbouring triangles. So, for every triangle three relative rotations connecting it with its neighbours can be generated. This encoding may seem wasteful as three rotations are stored instead of just one but this redundancy significantly improves the stability of the reconstruction when a deformation is applied to the encoded model. Additionally, on average only 1.5 rotations are stored as only one of $\mathbf{R}_{i,j}$ and $\mathbf{R}_{j,i}$ has to be stored. Recently, Kircher and Garland [57] have introduced a similar representation for editing mesh animations.

Reconstructing a mesh from this encoding involves solving two sparse linear systems. First we need to reconstruct $\mathbf{U}_i = \mathbf{R}_i \mathbf{S}_i$. Then, Poisson reconstruction yields the complete mesh. Creating the per-triangle rotations $\mathbf{R}_i$ from the relative rotations $\mathbf{R}_{i,j}$ requires solving a sparse linear system, which can be created by reordering Equation (4.1). For every set of neighbouring triangles equations of the form

$$\mathbf{R}_{i,j} \cdot \mathbf{R}_j - \mathbf{R}_i = 0 \tag{4.2}$$

are added to a sparse linear equation system. As long as the model is encoded and decoded without modification, the rotations $\mathbf{R}_i$ computed by solving this system are identical to the input, up to floating point accuracy and a global rotation. However, if any modification is applied to the encoded model, the resulting matrices $\mathbf{R}_i$ are not necessarily pure rotation matrices but may contain scale or shear components. To improve the stability of the reconstruction we perform matrix ortho-normalisation of the resulting $\mathbf{R}_i$ using singular value decomposition.

Now that a reversible procedure for encoding a model in a locally rotation invariant way has been described, we can think about how exactly the different components of the description are represented. The main requirement of the

FIGURE 4.1: Due to the relative rotation encoding (RRE) direct linear interpolation of two scans (left and right) results in realistic intermediate poses (middle right) whereas linear interpolation of vertex positions fails as can be seen, *e.g.*, in the subject's degenerated right arm (middle left).

encoding is that linear interpolation leads to intact representations. Shear matrices are already in a suitable format if only one half of the symmetric matrices are stored. Rotation matrices, however, are badly suited for direct interpolation. Evaluation of a number of different encodings leads directly to rotation vectors because this representation allows easy interpolation and unlike quaternions all possible combinations of values are valid and, in contrast to Euler Angles, the encoding does not suffer from gimbal lock [78]. Additionally, in order to further linearise the encoding space, all parameters are stored relative to the corresponding triangle of the mean model, which is constructed by averaging all components of all models in the relative encoding. The resulting final encoding has 10.5 degrees of freedom per triangle (4.5 for rotation and six for in-plane deformation).

The advantage of this complex representation is that it is hard to generate inconsistent meshes and that many common deformations, namely scaling during shape morphing and rotation during pose modification, are linear operations. This improves the quality of trained regression functions significantly and allows us to use linear regressors without visible loss of quality. As shown in Figure 4.1, it is even possible to linearly interpolate between two poses of a subject and obtain realistic results.

4.1. Rotational Invariance

Unfortunately, high frequency information, as present, for example, in the wrinkles of the pants the subjects are wearing, is very hard to represent with our model. Subjects sometimes adjust the fit of the pants between scans and the intra subject variance of wrinkles is even higher. So we opted to use a simple detail transfer procedure to re-add high frequency information after morphing, similar to displacement subdivision surfaces by Lee *et al.* [60]. This step improves firstly the accuracy of the estimated regression functions as noise is removed, secondly the efficiency since the computationally intensive steps operate on lower quality meshes, and thirdly the visual quality as high frequency information is retained during morphing instead of getting smoothed out. It works as follows: After fitting, the base mesh is subdivided using the simple mid-edge scheme and projected onto the scan. The offsets of the subdivision vertices in normal direction of the base mesh are stored with each triangle. During recall the mesh is subdivided again and the stored offsets are added.

4.1.1 Principal Component Analysis

Concatenating the rotations represented by rotation vectors and the components of the stretch matrices yields a high dimensional representation of human bodies that can be approximated linearly with respect to the most common deformations occurring in the combined body shape and pose space. Running principal component analysis (PCA) on the set of 3D scans yields a matrix of eigenvectors $\mathbf{E}$, describing the combined body shape and pose space and a set of low dimensional descriptors $\mathbf{x}$ of a scan $\mathbf{m}$ such that

$$\mathbf{m} = \mathbf{E} \cdot \mathbf{x} + \mathbf{a}, \tag{4.3}$$

where $\mathbf{m}$ is a model in the relative rotation encoding and $\mathbf{a}$ the average model. Every eigenvector of $\mathbf{E}$ corresponds to properties of the encoded human with different scales of influence on the body shape. However, if an unknown body shape is to be represented in the human body shape space a least squares system needs to be solved

$$\arg\min_{\mathbf{x}} \ (\mathbf{m} - \mathbf{E} \cdot \mathbf{x} + \mathbf{a})^2. \qquad (4.4)$$

In this naïve representation the influence of eigenvectors corresponding to small eigenvalues is overemphasised. This problem can be alleviated by dividing each eigenvector $\mathbf{e}_i$ by its eigenvalue e_i, yielding a matrix $\mathbf{W}$ of whitened coefficients (see [34]). In this new representation, every scaled eigenvector has the desired influence. Projecting a 3D model into the space of human shapes is equivalent to

$$\mathbf{x} = \mathbf{W}^+ \cdot (\mathbf{m} - \mathbf{a}), \qquad (4.5)$$

where $\mathbf{W}^+$ is the pseudo-inverse of $\mathbf{W}$. As a result of whitening the coefficients, the least-squares solution of Equation (4.5) results in a model $\mathbf{m}$ that is as close to the average human in a space that evenly describes all human traits as possible.

4.2 Splitting Shape and Pose

The elegant encoding introduced in the previous section describes pose and shape in a unified way. It even encodes correlations between the two. Unfortunately, for some applications it is necessary to control the components independently. In human motion capture, for example, it is known that the subject does not change from one frame to the next. Thus, it makes sense to keep the shape constant and allow only the pose to vary. In this section we present an approach that describes a 3D model as a sum of two components, one describing pose and one for shape.

Given a 3D model $\mathbf{m}_i$, encoded as described in Section 4.1, it can also be represented as a vector of PCA coefficients $\mathbf{x}_i$, given the whitened matrix of eigenvectors $\mathbf{W}$ and the average model $\mathbf{a}$

$$\mathbf{m}_i = \mathbf{W} \cdot \mathbf{x}_i + \mathbf{a}. \qquad (4.6)$$

4.2. Splitting Shape and Pose

The coefficients here specify pose and shape in an interdependent fashion. This is desirable in many applications because it allows the system to capture correlations between pose and shape. For markerless motion estimation, however, it is essential that pose and shape can be controlled separately, because body shape does not change significantly over the course of a sequence, whereas pose must be allowed to vary for every frame. We consequently propose to split the space spanned by the statistical model into a shape $\mathbf{S}$ and a pose $\mathbf{P}$ dependent space. So $\mathbf{m}_i$ can be represented by

$$\mathbf{m}_i = [\mathbf{S} \,|\, \mathbf{P}]\, \mathbf{x}'_i + \mathbf{a}. \tag{4.7}$$

By splitting the vector $\mathbf{x}'_i$ into two parts $\mathbf{x}'_i = [\mathbf{s}_i^\top \mathbf{p}_i^\top]^\top$, with shape $\mathbf{s}_i$ and pose $\mathbf{p}_i$, a consistent linear model of pose and shape can be generated. In order to compute $\mathbf{S}$ and $\mathbf{P}$ a linear system of equations is generated

$$\mathbf{M} = \mathbf{Z} \begin{bmatrix} \tilde{\mathbf{S}}^\top \\ \tilde{\mathbf{P}}^\top \end{bmatrix}, \tag{4.8}$$

where the matrix $\mathbf{M}$ comprises all scanned models $(\mathbf{m}_i - \mathbf{a})^\top$ as rows, and $\mathbf{Z}$ is a sparse matrix, where in each row the corresponding shape and pose are marked with a 1. In our case 114 subjects and for each model a subset of 55 possible poses are used. In total we use 532 input scans from the database. Solving the overdetermined system for $\tilde{\mathbf{S}}$ and $\tilde{\mathbf{P}}$ in the least-squares sense and performing PCA separately on $\tilde{\mathbf{S}}$ and $\tilde{\mathbf{P}}$ yields a set of variations of pose and shape sorted by relevance in the input dataset. In the resulting model 114 shape vectors and 55 pose vectors are retained. Finally, the Gram Schmidt algorithm [43] applied to $\begin{bmatrix}\tilde{\mathbf{S}} \,|\, \tilde{\mathbf{P}}\end{bmatrix}$ ensures that $\tilde{\mathbf{P}}$ spans a space orthogonal to $\tilde{\mathbf{S}}$. Consequently, assuming that $\mathbf{S}$ encodes all possible shape variations, pose transformations are unable to change the shape, because the relevant subspace does not overlap the space spanned by $\mathbf{S}$. The resulting variations of pose and shape are displayed in Figure 4.2. The observed shape variations are consistent with the literature [6]: Body height, weight, and gender cause the most significant changes in body

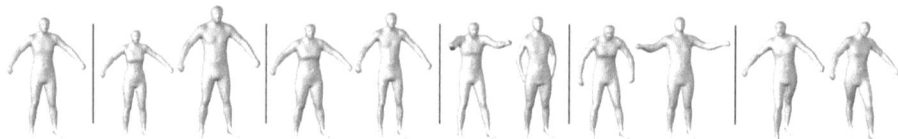

FIGURE 4.2: **Left to right**: The average model, the first two most significant shape variations, and the three most significant pose dependent eigenvectors (±2 standard deviations) are shown.

shape. The three most important changes in pose cause two different arm/upper body motions and a walking style leg motion.

4.3 Factorisation

In this section, we derive a method for estimating pose and shape parameters from registered 3D meshes of many subjects in many poses. The main idea of the approach presented here is that both shape and pose variations can be represented as affine transformations, and the vertices of each triangle can be explained by multiplication of the two transformation matrices. This is a bilinear model whose parameters – pose and shape – can be estimated by a linear, non-iterative procedure. The introduced algorithm is robust to missing scans, $i.e.$ not every subject has to be scanned in every pose. Furthermore, new meshes which are not in the database can be synthesised easily.

Assuming a bilinear model of pose and shape parameters implies that the vertices of each triangle can be factorised into

$$\mathbf{M}_{ijk} = \mathbf{P}_{ik}\mathbf{S}_{jk}\mathbf{T}. \tag{4.9}$$

Here, $\mathbf{M}_{ijk}$ is a 3×3 matrix consisting of the vertices of the kth triangle of subject j in pose i, and $\mathbf{T}$ is a canonical template triangle in the xy-plane. Matrices $\mathbf{P}$ and $\mathbf{S}$ are affine transformations applied to $\mathbf{T}$.

4.3. Factorisation

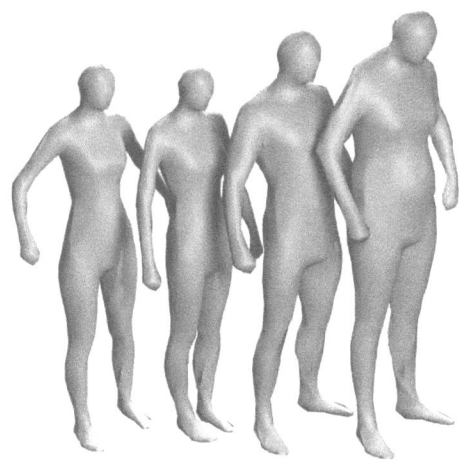

FIGURE 4.3: These subjects were asked to perform the same pose. Yet, variations in pose are significant.

The problem defined by Eq. (4.9) is to decompose $\mathbf{M}_{ijk}$ into pose and shape components $\mathbf{P}_{ik}$ and $\mathbf{S}_{jk}$, respectively. The classical factorisation algorithm [109] estimates them for all triangles of all scans simultaneously. Thereby, the constraint is imposed that pose i performed by one subject is identical to the same pose performed by a different subject. This implies that the differences between the two measurements are solely a result of body shape variations. Unfortunately, this prerequisite does not hold (cf. Fig. 4.3). Since individual poses vary, any algorithm must consider this during estimation. In the following, we will show that very few further assumptions are sufficient to obtain pose and shape parameters which satisfactorily explain the observed 3D meshes and which can be used to generate new 3D models not yet in the database.

The assumption that all poses of the individuals differ implies that each triangle $\mathbf{M}_{ijk}$ can be decomposed into a shape parameter $\mathbf{S}_{jk}$ and a shape-dependent pose parameter $\mathbf{P}_{ijk}$. The pose transformation $\mathbf{P}_{ijk}$ decomposes into a rotation matrix $\mathbf{R}_{ijk}$, and a deformation matrix $\mathbf{D}_{ijk}$ for shearing and scaling. Similarly, the shape transformation $\mathbf{S}_{jk}$ can be written as the product of a rotation $\mathbf{R}_{jk}$, and a shearing-scaling deformation $\mathbf{D}_{jk}$

$$\mathbf{P}_{ijk} = \mathbf{R}_{ijk}\mathbf{D}_{ijk} \quad \text{and} \quad \mathbf{S}_{jk} = \mathbf{R}_{jk}\mathbf{D}_{jk}. \tag{4.10}$$

Hence, $\mathbf{M}_{ijk}$ can be written as

$$\mathbf{M}_{ijk} = \mathbf{R}_{ijk}\mathbf{D}_{ijk}\mathbf{R}_{jk}\mathbf{D}_{jk}\mathbf{T}. \tag{4.11}$$

For every triangle $\mathbf{M}_{ijk}$ of subject j, shape parameters $\mathbf{R}_{jk}$ and $\mathbf{D}_{jk}$ are computed as the mean rotation and mean deformation over all poses of each subject.

Having estimated $\mathbf{S}_{jk}$ it seems that we may compute $\mathbf{P}_{ijk}$ simply as $\mathbf{P}_{ijk} = \mathbf{M}_{ijk}\mathbf{T}^+\mathbf{S}_{jk}^+$ where $(\cdot)^+$ denotes the generalised inverse. Unfortunately, if $\mathbf{P}_{ijk}$ is computed as described above, it cannot be applied to another subject. Simply transferring a pose of one subject to any other person violates the implicit assumption that triangles depend on the shape of the subject.

To generalise $\mathbf{P}_{ijk}$ so that it may be applied to other subjects, we introduce the constraint that deformations $\mathbf{D}_{ijk}$ always act on triangles in the xy-plane. This idea is motivated by the fact that shearing and scaling are not rotation-invariant. Therefore we define

$$\mathbf{D}'_{ik} = \mathbf{R}_{jk}^{-1}\mathbf{D}_{ik}\mathbf{R}_{jk} \tag{4.12}$$

and insert it into Eq. (4.11). This reverses the order of shape rotation $\mathbf{R}_{jk}$ and pose scaling $\mathbf{D}_{ijk}$ so that deformations always act on triangles in the xy-plane.

To be able to solve for $\mathbf{R}_{ijk}$ we need to further define

$$\mathbf{R}'_{ik} = \mathbf{R}_{jk}^{-1}\mathbf{R}_{ik}\mathbf{R}_{jk}. \tag{4.13}$$

Finally, we obtain

$$\mathbf{M}_{ijk} = \mathbf{P}_{ik}\mathbf{S}_{jk} = \mathbf{R}_{jk}\mathbf{R}'_{ik}\mathbf{D}'_{ik}\mathbf{D}_{jk}\mathbf{T}. \tag{4.14}$$

The decomposition of Eqs. (4.10) is performed by polar decomposition. However, whenever it is used care must be taken that the obtained rotation has a positive determinant. If the determinant of any rotation matrix happens to be negative, the sign of the right singular vector corresponding to the smallest singular value can be safely reversed since it only affects the unused deformation component in z-direction.

In summary, shape is computed as the average of all scans of a subject, and pose is considered to be a residual transformation. By immediately enforcing the various constraints during the estimation procedure, a separate correction step after factorisation becomes unnecessary[1].

Principal component analysis is finally employed to learn a lower dimensional model of the parameters of pose and shape bases. Pose and shape bases are used to explain the observed 3D mesh (*cf.* Sec. 6.1). This requires that a linear combination of pose and shape rotations is defined. Since this cannot be done directly with rotation matrices, we represent rotations as rotation vectors, which can be interpolated safely. We do similarly for the parameters of deformation. This is also motivated by a further compression, namely that rotation and deformation are reduced to only 3 parameters each.

4.4 Skeleton Based Description

In this section an approach for estimating rigid skeletons given a set of example meshes is detailed. The proposed method is able to estimate a combined linear blend skinning skeleton that changes shape and pose. In contrast to previous methods, the proposed approach allows controlling shape and pose independently.

---

[1] In fact, the factorisation algorithm as introduced in [109] estimates affinely distorted parameter sets. The original algorithm therefore requires a second stage called "metric upgrading" in which certain constraints are imposed on the model.

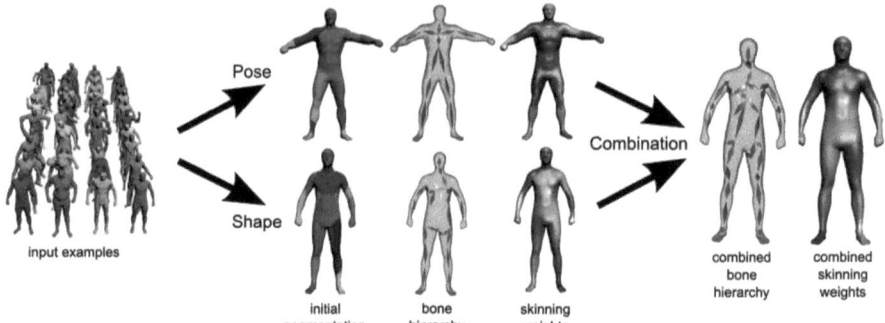

FIGURE 4.4: The overall optimisation pipeline is shown. Starting from a set of examples, different subjects in different poses, first an initial segmentation is computed with spectral clustering. Then, by iteratively solving for skinning weights and rotations/translations final skinning weights are generated. The transformations are used to compute the rigidity of potential connections between bones. The minimum spanning tree on this rigidity matrix, is equivalent to the corresponding hierarchy. If both, a pose and a shape skeleton are available, a combined skeleton can be used to control pose and shape of the mesh independently.

It is based on an elaborate optimisation procedure that can in the simplest case be split into five parts. Figure 4.4 visualises the involved steps. Firstly, a rough segmentation of the mesh into parts belonging to different bones is computed using spectral clustering (Sec. 4.4.1). Secondly, factorisation leads to initial skinning weights and estimates of the involved bone rotations and offsets (Sec. 4.3). In the third step, the bone hierarchy is computed by constructing the minimum spanning tree using joint location stability as the penalty function (Sec. 4.4.3). The joint locations are initialised to lie on the plane separating involved bones. An optimisation scheme then improves skinning weights and joint locations (Sec. 4.4.4). Finally, an optimal bind shape can be synthesised by solving a linear equation system (Sec. 4.4.5).

If scans from several subjects are given and both pose and shape are to be described by the skeleton, then, in order to preserve orthogonality of pose and shape, initially two skeletons are generated, one for shape and one for pose. These skeletons can be merged in a final step (Sec. 4.4.6). This allows pose and shape of a mesh to be controlled independently but with a joint representation.

4.4. Skeleton Based Description

4.4.1 Initialisation

One of our stated goals is to improve the skeleton estimation by incorporating several different subjects into the computation. The main idea to achieve this goal is that deformations between models are considered rather than using a global criterion. So by grouping the models according to subject, we can limit the observed deformations to pose dependent deformations while gathering information from several subjects.

Initially, the bind shapes for all subjects are computed using the relative rotation encoding proposed by [51]. Encoding all example models, computing the mean, and decoding the results leads to a suitable average model.

We further compute a rough initial segmentation of the mesh into rigid parts. Starting from a given template, we can compute the transformation $T_{i,e}$ into example e for every vertex i. Vertices that undergo similar transformations are moving rigidly. Considering only the rotational part $R_{i,e}$ of $T_{i,e}$ the angle between the transformations for vertices i and l can be computed by converting $R_{i,e} R_{l,e}^\top$ into a log-quaternion and computing its magnitude. This is a measure for the non-rigidness of the vertices. Spectral clustering (we use the self tuning variant [118]) of the resulting rigidity matrix leads to an initial segmentation into a specified number of body parts.

4.4.2 Factorisation

Linear blend skinning makes the assumption that a transformed vertex $\mathbf{p}'_i$ can be represented by the original vertex $\mathbf{p}_i$, the rotations $\mathbf{R}_j$ for each joint j, and scalar weights $w_{j,i}$, such that

$$\mathbf{p}'_i = \sum_j w_{j,i} (\mathbf{R}_j \cdot \mathbf{p}_i + \mathbf{v}_j), \tag{4.15}$$

where $\mathbf{v}_j$ is an additional offset that encodes the position of the joint centre. In our context, a number of these equations can be set up for each group of models belonging to one subject. Generally, it is possible to compare every model from a group with every other model from the group. However, if more than a few example models are considered, it becomes computationally intractable to consider all combinations. Since, the primary objective is to optimise the deformation starting from a single bind shape, it is sufficient to consider the transformations from bind shape to examples but not the transformations between different examples.

Since a first weight matrix $\mathbf{W}$ is available from the initial segmentation, we can rearrange Equation (4.15) and solve for $\mathbf{R}_j$ and $\mathbf{v}_j$. Unfortunately, the resulting matrices $\mathbf{R}_j$ are not necessarily orthonormal. This can be fixed by SVD based ortho-normalisation [53] but the resulting rotations may deviate significantly from the desired results. This situation can be improved by adding additional equations of the form

$$\mathbf{p}_i = \sum_j w_{j,i}(\mathbf{R}_j^{-1} \cdot \mathbf{p}'_i + \mathbf{v}'_j), \qquad (4.16)$$

where $\mathbf{v}'_j$ are additional offset vectors but $\mathbf{R}_j$ remains the same because $\mathbf{R}_j^\top = \mathbf{R}_j^{-1}$. The resulting matrices are very close to symmetric and the resulting ortho-normalisation is much closer to a reasonable rotation. Enforcing true rotation matrices leads to a non-linear cost function. Thus, the current result for $\mathbf{R}_j$, $\mathbf{v}_j$, and $\mathbf{v}'_j$ can be optimised further with the Levenberg-Marquardt algorithm [64].

In a second step we consider the rotations fixed and optimise the weight matrix. This can be done by solving a linear system, *e.g.*, with a non-negative least squares solver. However, this approach does not results in localised regions of influence of the bones. *I.e.* a bone may influence spatially distant regions, which can lead to unsightly artefacts. It also leads to many non-zero weights. [86] propose to perform segmentation on the weight map and keep only the most influential patch for each bone. Additionally, they cut off all non-zero influences

4.4. Skeleton Based Description

beyond the strongest four. This approach is easy to implement and seems to work. Yet, it may be desirable to have one joint control two limbs if they are always moving synchronously and the limit of four influences seems, apart from efficiency reasons when implementing LBS on graphics hardware, arbitrary.

In contrast, we opt to introduce an additional constraint into the optimisation. Namely, the $L1$-norm of the weight matrix, which induces sparseness, is minimised simultaneously. This optimisation target is obviously in conflict with the constraint $\sum_j w_{j,i} = 1$. However, as the sum of weights constraint is minimised in the least squares sense while sparsity is enforced with the $L1$-norm, after renormalisation, the result is still more sparse than a non-negative least squares solution. We use the implementation provided by [119]. After about 10 iterations of solving for rotations and weights the method converges and we can continue by computing a hierarchy of bones.

4.4.3 Hierarchy Generation

The bone rotations and translations computed in the previous step cannot be transformed directly into a skeleton hierarchy because the offset vectors $\mathbf{v}_j$ are not necessarily consistent with the intrinsic joint hierarchy. This can easily be seen if we consider the following: The position of point $\mathbf{p}_1$ after rotating it by $\mathbf{R}_0$ around point $\mathbf{p}_0$ is determined by

$$\mathbf{p}'_1 = \mathbf{R}_0 \cdot (\mathbf{p}_1 - \mathbf{p}_0) + \mathbf{p}_0 = \mathbf{R}_0 \mathbf{p}_1 + \underbrace{\mathbf{p}_0 - \mathbf{R}_0 \mathbf{p}_1}_{\mathbf{v}_0}. \tag{4.17}$$

The optimisation, performed in Section 4.3, employs Equation (4.15), and allows $\mathbf{v}_j$ to be chosen freely. This additional degree of freedom effectively allows the optimisation to freely move the joint centres for every example. However, due to the underlying assumption that the 3D models consist mostly of rigidly moving body parts, we can nonetheless use the estimates to compute connectivity and rough positions of the true joint centres. The basic insight that, given two connected bones j and k, the connecting joint centre $\mathbf{j}_{j,k}$ is invariant with respect to the child bone's rotation, leads to

$$\mathbf{R}_j \mathbf{j}_{j,k} + \mathbf{v}_j = \mathbf{R}_k \mathbf{j}_{j,k} + \mathbf{v}_k. \tag{4.18}$$

Thus, given a number of observations $\mathbf{R}_n, \mathbf{v}_n$, the joint centre can be determined by solving the overdetermined system of equations

$$(\mathbf{R}_{j,n} - \mathbf{R}_{k,n})\mathbf{j}_{j,k} = \mathbf{v}_{k,n} - \mathbf{v}_{j,n} \tag{4.19}$$

for $\mathbf{j}_{j,k}$. Determining the residual error leads to a measure of the connectedness of two bones [86]. Computing the full connectedness graph and finding the minimum spanning tree [59] leads to an optimal skeleton hierarchy.

Determining the root node is mostly a question of ease of use for a human modeller. For optimisation purposes it is not really relevant. A human, however, expects the root to be lie near the perceived centre of the model. We accordingly choose the *graph centre* [45] as the root node.

4.4.4 Joint Position Estimation

The main challenge when determining joint centres lies with hinge joints because the joint centre of a hinge joint can lie anywhere on the hinge axis. Of course in real world examples with measurement inaccuracies and non-rigid deformation this case cannot be detected by Eigenanalysis of the rotation matrices, which would be a good indicator in the ideal case. The joint centres computed with Equation (4.19), however, exhibit the described artefact. The points lie anywhere on the approximate hinge axis. Again, the skeletons are fully functional but the human modeller expects the bones to lie within the surface of the model. So we initialise the joint centres by placing them on the

4.4. Skeleton Based Description

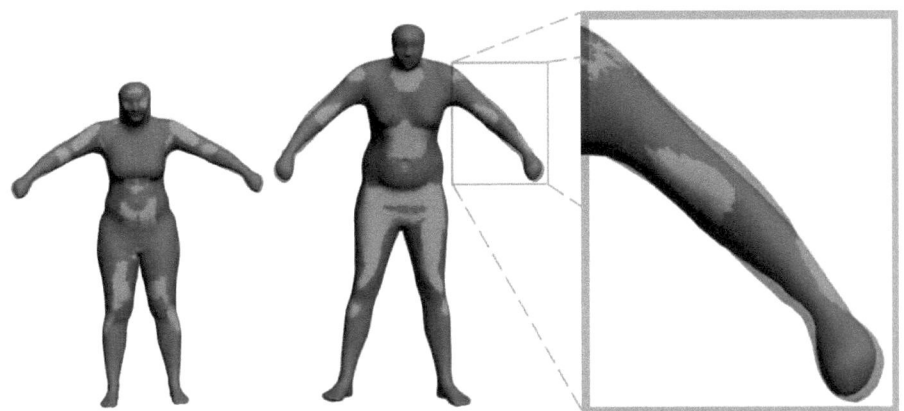

FIGURE 4.5: Comparison of the initial bind shape (red) and the improved bind shape (green) for a female and male example (with detail magnification)

interface between the two involved bones using the equation provided by [86]

$$\mathbf{j} = \frac{\sum_i \min(w_{i,1}, w_{i,2}) \mathbf{p}_i}{\sum_i \min(w_{i,1}, w_{i,2})}, \quad (4.20)$$

where $\mathbf{p}_i$ are all vertices with non-zero weights for the two bones. Afterwards, the positions $\mathbf{j}$ are refined with a Levenberg-Marquardt gradient descent scheme, optimising Equation (4.15), which can be expressed as a non-linear function of $\mathbf{j}$. It also proved beneficial to repeat the skinning weight optimisation from Section 4.3 after updating the joint positions.

4.4.5 Bind Shape Synthesis

In a final step, the bind shape of the model can be optimised. So far, all existing approaches have used an arbitrary example as the bind shape. This model is typically chosen manually. In contrast, in our method, the initial bind shape is the average model generated using the relative rotation encoding (*cf.* Section 4.4.1). It is easy to improve on this, however, by solving the overdetermined system of linear equations resulting from Equation (4.15) for $\mathbf{p}_i$ (*cf.* Figure 4.5).

4.4.6 Combining Shape and Pose

The above procedure describes a method for generating a skeleton given a set of example models. With it, we can create skeletons for changing either pose or shape. Yet, it is not feasible to directly create a combined model of pose and shape that separates the contributions of shape and pose. This would be of great importance for simple manual animation of the resulting skeleton. In this section an approach is introduced for generating such a combined skeleton starting from two skeletons, one describing pose and one for shape.

Firstly, a shape deformation skeleton is computed, using models of different persons each scanned in a similar rest pose using the approach described above. The generated skeleton is then used to recreate the subjects in their rest poses. Secondly, these models derived with the shape skeleton serve as bind shapes for the second skeleton, which describes pose variations. Since the two skeletons are coupled via the bind poses, a combined skeleton can be created by performing the two transformations one after the other. So, similar to Equation (4.15), the combined transformation can be expressed as

$$\mathbf{p}'_i = \left(\sum_j w^s_{j,i}(\mathbf{R}^s_j + \mathbf{v}^s_j)\right) \cdot \left(\sum_j w^p_{j,i}(\mathbf{R}^p_j + \mathbf{v}^p_j)\right) \cdot \mathbf{p}_i. \qquad (4.21)$$

In this formulation every shape bone influences every pose bone. This is undesirable because the resulting graph structure is highly connected, whereas common graphics packages can only handle tree structures. Consequently, it is necessary to simplify the graph to a tree. This is an approximation to the real structure but since the areas of influence of the bones are highly localised, most bones don't overlap significantly. The corresponding factors can consequently be dropped. Since the weight matrices of the skeletons describe the areas of

4.4. Skeleton Based Description

influence, it is clear that the multiplication of the two results in a merit function that clusters bones by their area of influence. By concatenating the two weight functions $\mathbf{W}_c = [\mathbf{W}_s, \mathbf{W}_p]$, a general merit matrix $\mathbf{M}$ can be computed.

$$\mathbf{M} = \mathbf{W}_c^\top \mathbf{W}_c \qquad (4.22)$$

Similar to Section 4.4.3, the minimum spanning tree leads to a reasonable tree structure fitted into the graph. In the given problem, however, additional constraints have to be respected. Namely, it is essential that the hierarchy of the original skeletons is preserved. A joint a that is a child (direct or indirect) of joint b in a shape skeleton has to remain a child of joint b in the combined hierarchy. It is admissible, however, to introduce additional nodes between a and b as long as they are from the pose skeleton. The reverse delete algorithm for computing the minimum spanning tree [59] can be modified to incorporate this type of constraint. Unfortunately, after the modified algorithm terminates, some small cycles can remain. These cycles are dissolved by connecting the involved nodes fully and rerunning the above modified reverse delete algorithm. This time, however, only the pose hierarchy is enforced. Since these cycles normally appear in the chest region, near the root of the tree, violations of the shape hierarchy which primarily performs translation and only little rotation are not vital. In the resulting skeletons pose and shape bones frequently alternate because the constraints allow only insertion of nodes from the respective other skeleton (*cf.* Fig. 4.6).

4.4.7 Translation vs. Scaling

Since the articulated motion of humans can be described well by distinct rigid body motions with blending, skeleton based systems describing rotation and translation for every bone are very successful. Shape changes, on the other hand, can be explained more easily by a hierarchy of scale and rotation transformations. Thus, for shape describing skeletons we incorporate additional

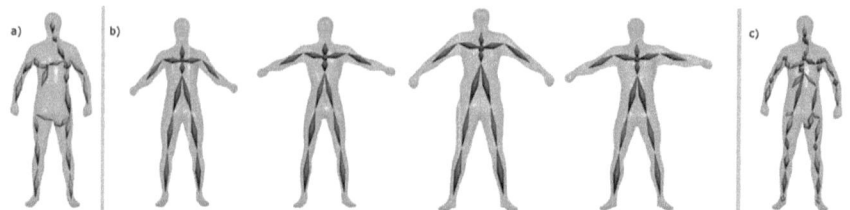

FIGURE 4.6: A shape skeleton **a)** and pose skeleton for different subjects that were estimated simultaneously **b)** are merged into a combined pose and shape skeleton **c)**. In the combined skeleton the hierarchy of the pose skeleton is enforced. Since shape skeletons are not as sensitive to changes in the hierarchy, the shape hierarchy is allowed to be broken if no overall consistent tree can be found.

terms into Equation (4.15)

$$\mathbf{p}'_i = \sum_j w_{j,i}(\mathbf{R}_j \mathbf{S}_j \cdot \mathbf{p}_i + \mathbf{v}_j), \qquad (4.23)$$

where $\mathbf{S}_j$ is a diagonal matrix and $\mathbf{v}_j$ does not encode any translation beyond the initial offset of a joint relative to its parent. The optimisation strategy described above has to be adjusted accordingly but the necessary changes are straight-forward. Figure 4.7 shows the difference in quality that can be achieved when computing a shape skeleton with translation or scaling.

A significant disadvantage of incorporating scale into a skeleton hierarchy is that it invariably introduces shearing in dependent nodes during articulation. This effect is not substantial if all examples are in approximately the same pose but can introduce serious artefacts during pose animation. The artefact can be avoided by performing the scaling in the untransformed coordinate system of the bone, $i.e.$, the transformation $\mathbf{T}_a$ of bone a, which is a child of bone b can be written as

$$\mathbf{T}_a = \mathbf{R}_a \mathbf{R}_b \mathbf{S}_a \mathbf{R}_b^\top, \qquad (4.24)$$

where $\mathbf{R}$ and $\mathbf{S}$ denote rotation and scale matrices, respectively. Unfortunately, this non-standard approach is not generally supported. Since the difference between the shape described by translation and that described by scaling is not

4.4. Skeleton Based Description

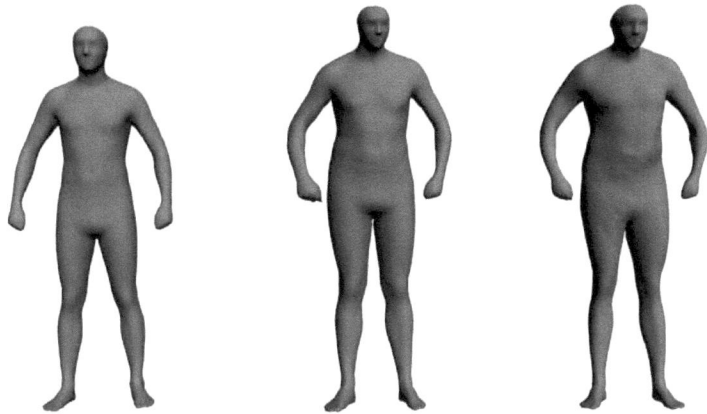

FIGURE 4.7: Transforming a bind shape (left) to another shape using a shape skeleton that allows rotation and scale (middle) in comparison with a shape skeleton that allows rotation and translation (right).

significant, as shown in Figure 4.7, we instead opt to allow translation instead of scaling during shape skeleton construction.

4.4.8 Estimation Error

In this section experiments are described that show the effectiveness of the approach presented in the previous section. We start by showing results exploring the classic pipeline for estimating a pose dependent skeleton (the top branch in Figure 4.4). Then, new poses of the combined shape and pose model are shown.

As described above, the bind shape is first approximated by the rotation invariant mean of the examples and refined by solving a linear equation system as the last step of the pipeline. A comparison of the two is shown in Figure 4.5. Although the differences are subtle, slightly more detail is visible in the refined shape and the numerical error is significantly (for the horse on average 11%) smaller.

Final results for the three single entity sets are shown in Figures 4.9, 4.10, and 4.11. They show the refined bind shapes, the input meshes used during optimisation, the estimated skeletons, skinning weights, and a few poses not present in the input sets. Of course, the input sequences used for these three models were generated with similar methods as the technology underlying our approach. It may consequently be unsurprising that it is possible to achieve accurate results with it. The human dataset, however, was obtained by registering 3D scans of real persons to a template mesh. So the assumptions we make (all deformations are based on a rigid skeleton) are only approximately true. The results we obtain are nonetheless as good as for the synthetic sequences.

Table 4.1 summarises the residual root mean squared errors (RMSE) for recreating the input examples as a function of the number of bones for the male and female models, as well as the horse and the cat. As shown, the accuracy is comparable to other recent methods [30, 86]. It is also interesting to note that, despite the gross simplification introduced by merging the skeletons (*cf.* Sec. 4.4.6), the error for the combined model is not significantly higher than that of the solely shape or pose dependent models.

Since the final model does not use any non-standard techniques, it is possible to load the resulting skinned mesh into common modelling packages. Figure 4.8 shows the horse model posed in 3D Studio Max.

For symmetric shapes, a user might expect the algorithm to find a symmetric skeleton. Yet, the only symmetrisation we currently perform is, that for the humans, we add mirrored versions of the examples to the input set. The resulting pose skeletons are frequently fairly symmetric but the shape skeletons are not. This is probably related to the fact that, since shape skeletons are mostly controlled by translation, the exact hierarchy of the bones is not as important as for pose skeletons. The undesired translation of a parent node can then be compensated for by translating in the opposite direction, which is not possible for rotations. Nonetheless, it would be possible and easy to enforce symmetric skinning weights, and joint positions for either type of skeleton.

4.4. Skeleton Based Description

model	S	N	RMSE (%)				
# Bones			10	11	12	13	14
pose (men)	4	80	0.70	0.62	0.61	0.59	0.57
pose (women)	6	120	0.66	0.61	0.60	0.61	0.56
# Bones			10	15	20	25	30
shape (men)	59	118	0.48	0.41	0.37	0.34	0.32
shape (women)	55	110	0.54	0.45	0.41	0.37	0.35
# Bones				34	39	44	
combined (men)	59	190		1.12	0.88	0.96	
combined (women)	55	218			0.88	0.92	
# Bones			10	15	20	25	
horse	1	12	0.90	0.56	0.51	0.38	
# Bones			12	13	14	15	
cat	1	8	1.45	1.20	1.16	1.02	

TABLE 4.1: The residual RMSE normalised by the bounding volume diagonal is shown as a function of the number of joints. **S** denotes the number of subjects and **N** the number of examples. The shape model and the combined model allow rotation and translation of the bones only.

The presented approach is limited in that it can only estimate bones if the relative motion is non-zero in at least one example. If, for example, in a set of meshes the arms of a subject move in parallel, it is impossible for the algorithm to determine that two bones are required. A user may, on the other hand, expect that the prongs of a forklift are controlled by a single bone. Distinguishing these two cases is, in the general case, difficult. An additional limitation of the method is that when combining shape and pose skeletons, the correlations between pose and shape are lost. This effect cannot be avoided unless the commitment to a strict skeleton hierarchy with LBS is dropped.

Despite these limitations, a powerful method for converting a sparse set of examples into a fully rigged kinematic skeleton, has been presented.

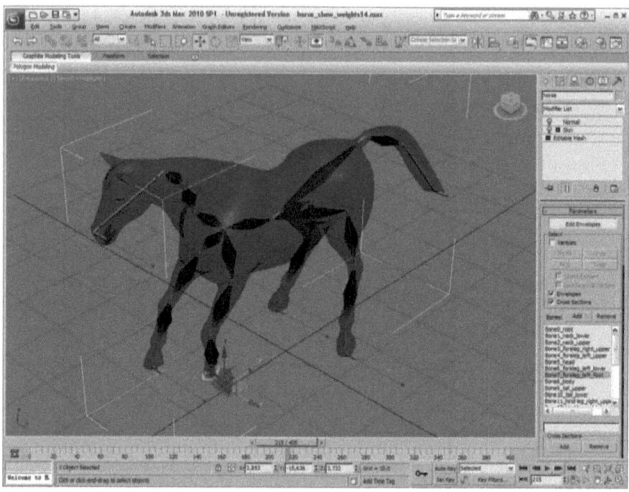

FIGURE 4.8: The final model is compatible with current 3D modelling tools and game engines. Here, the horse is posed in 3D Studio Max.

4.5 Discussion

In this chapter four representations for general models of human pose and shape are presented. Although all presented approaches solve the same problem, emphasis is placed on different aspects and applications.

The first approach is aimed at high quality synthesis. This model is able to model muscle deformations and even their correlations to body shape, *i.e.*, muscles deform differently depending on the markedness of skeletal musculature of the modelled subject. Secondly, a derivative model is introduced, which allows controlling shape and pose parameters independently. This is advantageous, *e.g.*, in a markerless motion capture context because here, it is known that the body shape of the tracked subject is unchanged, while the pose varies every frame. However, this increase in controllability comes at a cost. The correlations between muscle deformation and shape are lost. Only generic muscle deformations can be represented.

4.5. Discussion

FIGURE 4.9: **Top:** input examples, **Middle** (left to right): bind shape, segmentation, extracted bone skeleton, **Bottom:** new poses generated with the extracted skeleton.

The factorisation-based method is also unable to capture correlations between pose and shape but global muscle deformation, as present, *e.g.*, in the SCAPE model can also be represented. This approach has the advantage that the synthesis of 3D meshes is computationally cheaper and in the context of vision-based shape matching it converges more stably than the above methods.

Finally, a description based on linear blend skinning is presented. Unlike the

FIGURE 4.10: **Top:** input examples, **Middle** (left to right): bind shape, segmentation, extracted bone skeleton, **Bottom:** new poses generated with the extracted skeleton.

other approaches, the representation itself is not a contribution. On the contrary, linear blend skinning is the industry standard for real-time mesh animation. The contribution here is the approach for computing a linear blend skinning skeleton that is able to represent both shape and pose variations. Since the resulting representation uses linear blend skinning only, a system for real-time synthesis of generic humans in arbitrary shapes and poses, compatible with most common modelling packages and game engines, is presented.

Applications of these models are presented in the following chapters (Ch. 5 and 6) and a comparison of all methods on a morphing task is offered in Section 5.1.

4.5. Discussion

FIGURE 4.11: **Top:** input examples, **Middle** (left to right): bind shape, segmentation, extracted bone skeleton, **Bottom:** new poses generated with the extracted skeleton.

> How do you distinguish between being
> off-route and putting up a first ascent?
> BRUCE BINDNER

Chapter 5

Generative Applications

Using the shape descriptions developed in the previous chapter many applications can be realised. These applications can be grouped roughly into two categories: generative and estimative. Generative methods are used to synthesise new shapes just given semantic constraints or by morphing a template, for example, for animation purposes. The expressiveness of these methods also shows their general applicability to vision tasks/estimation applications because the analysis-by-synthesis approaches, applied there, generate successively more accurate results and the accuracy of an estimate depends significantly on the expressiveness of the underlying shape model.

This chapter focuses on generative applications. In particular, different morphing and deformation approaches are presented (Sec. 5.1 to 5.4), followed by two section on animation. In the first section a morphing task is performed with all models described in the previous chapter. This shows that similar results can be obtained with any of the described methods. Yet, since the differential rotation encoding, described in Section 4.1, achieves the highest quality, all but the last section apply this model, trusting that similar results could be obtained with any of the models. In the last section (Sec. 5.6) results using the real-time animatable model from Section 4.4 are shown.

5.1 Morphing

Morphing is the most basic application that can be performed with any shape model. On its own it may not even be considered an application. Yet, it is essential to show that this most basic operation works well for all approaches to lay the foundation for more complex applications. Figure 5.1 shows the three models side-by-side performing the same morphing functions. The results of the relative encoding (left) and its derivative with direct control of the pose (middle) are almost identical. Only using the split model the pose of the top subject is replicated in the middle row. This is not possible with the simple relative encoding. On the right, the factorisation approach is shown. These results are less detailed because the model has been computed on lower resolution meshes only. Overall, the visual quality of all morphs is high. All meshes look convincingly realistic. The detail of the factorisation model is lower because in order to increase its speed lower resolution meshes were used to train the model. However, its primary application is in vision tasks and it is doubtful that these tasks would benefit from higher resolution meshes. Only the perceived detail of the results would be higher. These details, however, would mostly stem from the training data instead of truly being estimated from image data.

5.2 Semantic Constraints

In addition to simple shape or pose interpolation, it is interesting to introduce semantic constraints. It may, for example, be necessary to generate a large number of male humans with certain height constraints. Enforcing a single constraint is fairly straight forward. If measurements of some semantic variable $\mathbf{v}$ are available for every subject i, a linear system can be set up that correlates PCA coefficients with $\mathbf{v}$.

$$\begin{bmatrix} \mathbf{1} \mathbf{A}^\top \end{bmatrix} \mathbf{f} = \mathbf{v} \tag{5.1}$$

5.2. Semantic Constraints

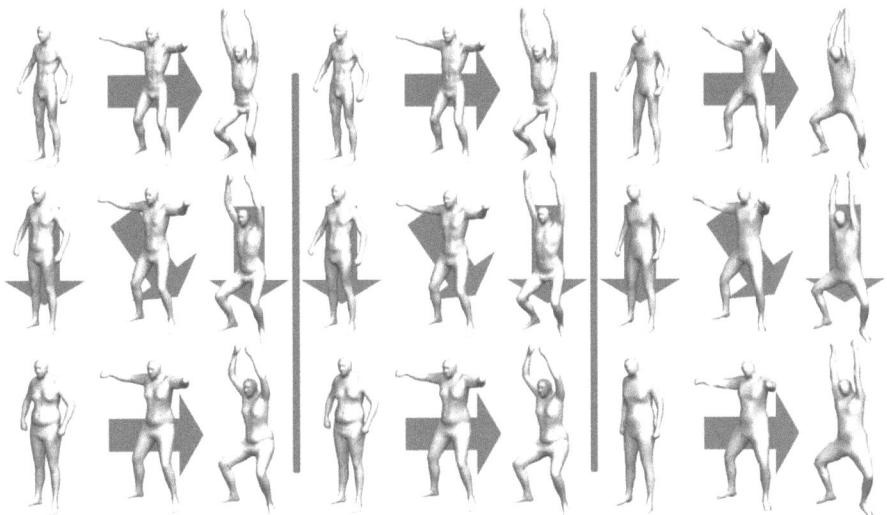

FIGURE 5.1: The three different shape descriptions are compared on a simple morphing task. The corners of the squares show input data while the inner meshes are generated from the neighbours indicated by the arrows. **Left to right**: The relative rotation encoding, the split relative encoding, and the factorisation method are shown. Please note that for the split relative encoding (middle column) the pose of the top subject is replicated in the middle row, whereas on the left the poses in the middle column are interpolated between top and bottom. The morphs based on the factorisation model were computed on a lower resolution mesh.

Here, $\mathbf{A}$ is the matrix of shapes projected into human shape/pose space and $\mathbf{f}$ denotes a vector describing the learned linear function. Enforcing the constraint, given an input mesh can then be achieved by projecting the mesh first into the PCA space and then solving an underdetermined linear system in the minimum norm sense for the necessary offset δ

$$\left[1(\mathbf{x}^\top + \delta^\top)\right] \mathbf{f} = c. \tag{5.2}$$

Here, c denotes the prescribed value for the given semantic constraint and $\mathbf{x}$ is the input mesh's representation in the space of human shapes and poses.

5.2.1 Semantic Model Basis

In addition, it is interesting to rotate the original PCA basis such that the first vectors correspond to semantically meaningful directions since this allows morphing a subject while keeping some constraints constant. For example, increasing body height normally results in additional weight. However, by keeping weight constant while increasing height, results in progressively slimmer subjects.

The Gram-Schmidt algorithm [43] is used to span the subspace of the original PCA space such that it is orthogonal to all given semantic morphing vectors. Then PCA is used to generate a basis for the remaining subspace. The new basis and all morphing vectors now span the original PCA space. Thereafter, all scans are transformed to the new base. The reconstruction of these models using only the subspace not spanned by semantic variables leads to a representation in which all models are invariant to the semantic constraint variables. The PCA of these reconstructions in combination with the semantic constraint vectors represents the final basis. The desirable properties of this basis are that the first vectors directly represent semantically meaningful gradient directions and the remaining human body shape space is spanned by a PCA basis. By applying Gram-Schmidt on the semantic vectors as well and normalising their lengths, we can enforce orthonormality of the transformation. A mixing matrix and scale factors can be used to directly specify semantically meaningful constraints. However, in most cases this step is unnecessary because the semantic constraints are held constant at specific values and solving of linear systems is only performed on the remaining subspace. So minimum norm solutions behave as expected.

5.2. Semantic Constraints

Regressor	Height	Weight	Body Fat	Muscles	Waist
simple linear	3.68	3.03	3.38	5.63	2.78
filtered linear	1.43	1.33	2.02	2.41	0.945
non-linear	1.15	1.17	1.66	2.38	0.858

TABLE 5.1: Root mean squared errors estimated by 10-fold cross validation for different semantic variables and regressors on a model that contains every subject exactly once. Weight is measured in kg, Body Fat, and Muscles in %, and Height and Waist Girth in cm.

5.2.2 Evaluation

In line with research conducted by Allen *et al.* [3] and Seo and Magnenat-Thalmann [93] we present body shape morphing driven by high level semantic variables. We also conduct quantitative analysis of the accuracy of the trained functions. In Table 5.1 mean squared errors generated by 10-fold cross validation of different semantic functions are presented. It is doubtful that changes within the range of these error bounds are perceptible when the corresponding meshes are rendered. The data also shows that, as a result of the non-linear relative rotation encoding, the achievable accuracy is only slightly better when using non-linear rather than linear regression. This assumption is confirmed by the observations summarised in Table 5.2. Mean and standard deviation of the angles between morphing directions for selected functions computed for all subjects in the shape-only model are shown. All of these values are small indicating that morphing directions are highly collinear independent of the position in shape space. Apparently, the relative rotation encoding linearises the space sufficiently so that it is now admissible to use a linear function to represent the changes.

Unfortunately, many semantically meaningful functions cannot easily be evaluated quantitatively. For example, in order to define a muscledness function the subjects in the database have to be labelled somehow. Yet, it is hard for a human judge to assign a number to the muscledness of a person. It is much easier to compare two given scans and decide on the more muscled subject. Each random pairing of scans defines a gradient direction. The judge only chooses

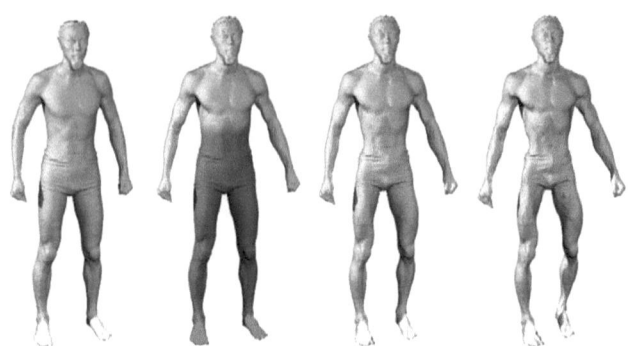

FIGURE 5.2: The effects of applying the muscledness function. **Left to right**: Original, a selective mask was applied to increase only upper body muscles, full body muscle augmentation, and an extremely muscular caricature.

	Height	Weight	Body Fat	Waist Girth
μ	2.04	1.47	2.78	2.00
σ	0.688	0.520	0.853	0.715

TABLE 5.2: Mean and standard deviation of angles (in degrees) between morphing directions computed by the non-linear model for all subjects.

the sign of the gradient towards greater muscularity. By first normalising and then averaging the gradients, a general muscularity function can be generated. Results of applying the function are shown in Figure 5.2.

Since morphing functions can operate directly on the relative encoding, it is trivial to constrain morphing to selected body parts. A multiplicative mask allows deformation to occur in selected areas. The reconstruction process spreads out the error arising at the edge of the selected region evenly, preventing the development of steps in the surface. Figure 5.2 shows selective morphing of the upper body using the muscledness function.

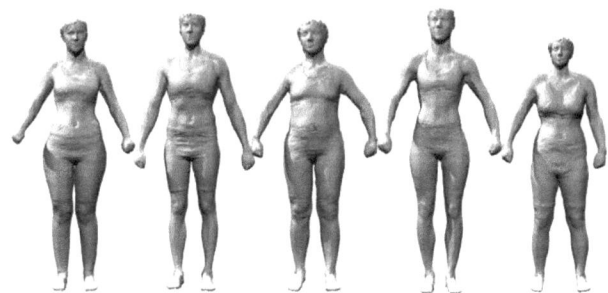

FIGURE 5.3: Several women were randomly generated using the semantic basis. We applied the constraints sex = female and weight = 65 kg. As expected the taller the woman the slimmer she is.

5.3 Character Generation

As shown recently, it is essential for the perception of the diversity of a crowd that the body shapes of the characters differ significantly [66]. It is consequently important to have a simple method that allows the generation of diverse body shapes. Yet, it may also be important to be able to tightly control a generated character's body shape. Employing our model both objectives can be achieved by combining two different approaches.

The PCA projects the largest variances of a dataset in the first components while noise like features are displaced to the last components. This is a most welcome feature for many applications. For the purpose of generating a random character that exhibits a unique physique while creating a natural, human look, a PCA based shape-only model is the tool of choice. We use a model consisting only of scans of subjects in the resting pose. The model that contains all scans cannot be used for this purpose since it contains pose dependent components in the first PCA vectors. So, a randomly generated character with the limited model would exhibit not just changes in shape but also in pose. Yet, for animation the generated characters can be plugged directly into the full model as described in Section 5.5.

The advantage of the PCA based technique is that the diversity of the generated characters is very high. On the downside, control over the type of generated character is fairly low. Neither gender nor body weight or height can easily be controlled as the PCA vectors do not, unlike often assumed, directly pertain to a single semantically relevant measure. We can, however, take a given starting point, generated, *e.g.*, with the above technique and apply the morphing described in Section 5.1 to enforce a given set of constraints. Unfortunately, this approach, although workable, may produce suboptimal results since the morphed distance may be large, introducing artifacts on the way.

It is much more efficient to use the semantic basis introduced in Section 5.2.1. This technique allows us to specify semantic constraints such as height between 1.70 m and 1.90 m and sex between 0.9 and 1.1 male and allow the system to fill in the details. Ultimately, this approach is used to generate the models displayed in Figure 5.3 whereas Figure 5.4 shows a crowd that was generated without constraints.

5.4 Handle Based Body Shape Modelling

Additional adjustments may be deemed necessary by the responsible artist. Obviously morphing along semantic trajectories is a simple option. In this section a different approach is introduced. By adding moveable handles to the body model a very intuitive way of changing body shape is established. This avenue is opened by our use of Poisson reconstruction in the last step which allows the inclusion of additional positional constraints. The deformation that is required to conform to the constraints is distributed evenly. In fact, mesh editing has been performed using this technique [116]. However, we want the constraints to influence the body shape realistically instead of just deforming the initial shape in the least squares sense because this inevitably leads to unrealistic distortions. This, however, can easily be mended by projecting the candidate body model into the PCA space spanned by the body shape database since

5.4. Handle Based Body Shape Modelling

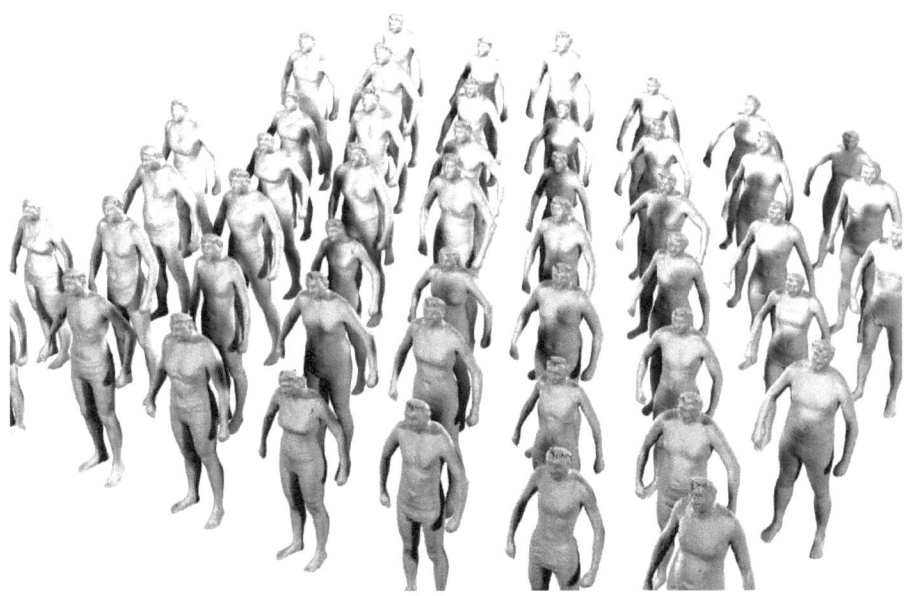

FIGURE 5.4: An example of a randomly generated set of characters.

primarily valid body models can be represented in this space. It may thus not be possible to represent the proposed model in shape-space and constraints are not met exactly. So, we iterate between deforming the model and projecting it back into the space of body shapes. After about 10 iterations the system converges. Still, the method acts as a very strong regulariser, so that constraints are frequently not met exactly and it may be necessary to exaggerate them to achieve a desired effect. A simple editing session is shown in Figure 5.5.

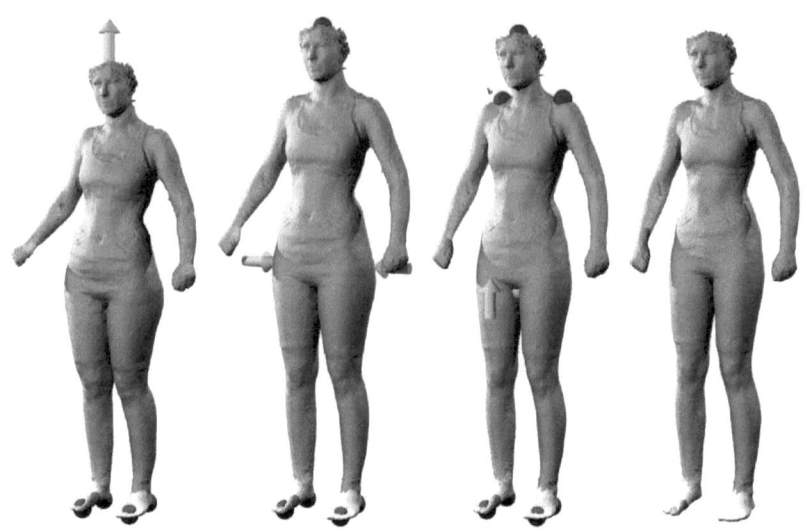

FIGURE 5.5: A handle based interface for editing body shapes. The red markers are held in place while the yellow arrows show where attached markers are moved. First the height is increased, then hip width is decreased, and last the crotch is raised.

5.5 Animation

Every scan's pose is estimated during registration. Thus we can easily train functions that each change a specific degree of freedom of the pose. That way, we can morph any scan into a specified pose. Since animations are frequently parameterised by a set of joint angles for every frame, we can simply morph a given model to conform to these constraints to animate it. This works well for most joints and poses.

However, improvements are possible if two minor issues are addressed. Some functions' areas of influence are not localised to the expected area but also include areas on the mirrored side of the body. This is a result of the choice of scanned poses. In most poses arm movements are symmetric. Fortunately, the effect can be compensated for by computing some functions, namely all functions concerning arm movement, only on one side of the body. Similarly, it proved beneficial to split PCA vectors into left and right halfs during reprojection of candidate models to assist independent motion of left and right arms.

Furthermore, absolute positioning accuracy of end effectors can be improved by following Wang *et al.* [112] who propose to add positional constraints to the tips of limbs during the Poisson reconstruction step. This step also serves to correct correlations that were wrongly learned. For example, in one of the poses the subjects stand on one leg (*cf*. Fig. 3.3). In order to keep balance and not to move for the 10 s it takes to perform the scan a very unrelaxed upper body posture was commonly adopted by the subjects. This has led to undesired correlations. Also note that these artifacts cannot be prevented unless fast 3D scanning of moving subjects is performed, which is not available today at a comparable accuracy. A side-by-side comparison of using end effector constraints vs. not using them is shown in Figure 5.6. Figure 5.7 shows several frames from an animation. In one of the frames the subject crosses his legs. This is significant as no pose of a scan in the database is even close to the displayed pose. A subject is morphed into a pose that is not in the database and compared to a scan in a similar pose in Fig. 5.8. Additionally, a person who is not in the database is represented by our model.

5.6 Real-time Animation

Using the skeleton based model both pose and shape can be changed in real-time. Selected morphing results are presented here. Figure 5.9 shows two shape skeletons, one describing female body shape and one for males and three pose skeletons for different subjects. Each is shown in two significantly different poses/shapes. Exemplary results of the merge of pose and shape skeletons are shown in Figure 5.10. Here a woman walks and simultaneously changes body shape.

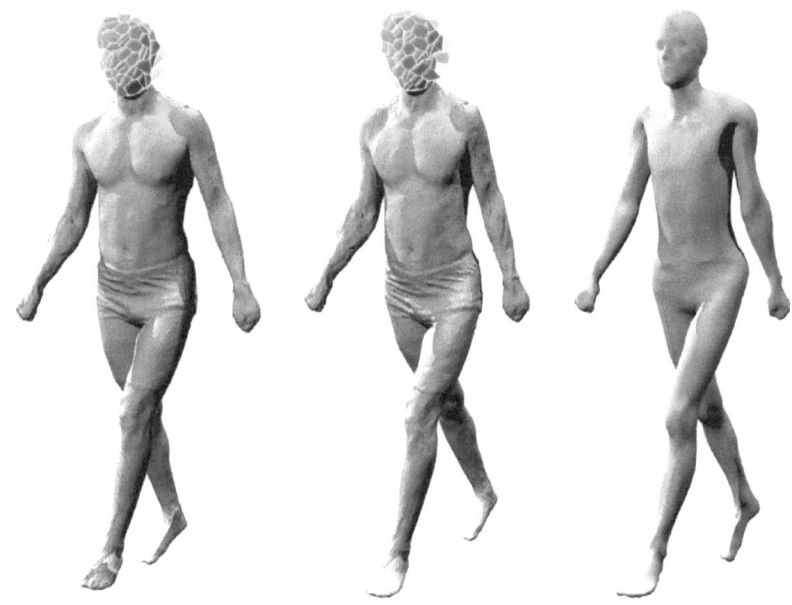

FIGURE 5.6: By adding positional constraints during reconstruction of deformed models it is possible to ameliorate accumulated pose errors. Here the effect of using positional constraints is demonstrated. **Left**: No constraints, **Middle**: Constraints, **Right**: Reference Pose.

5.7 Discussion

In this chapter, animation related applications of the different models are explored. For the most part only the differential rotation encoding is employed. However, the deformation methods can be applied analogously to the other models.

One particularly interesting conclusion that can be drawn from this chapter is that even complex functions such as perceived muscularity or measured physical properties can be approximated well by linear functions. Although, artefacts are to be expected when shapes far from the mean shape are morphed. This favourable property is probably a result of the differential rotation encoding as

5.7. Discussion

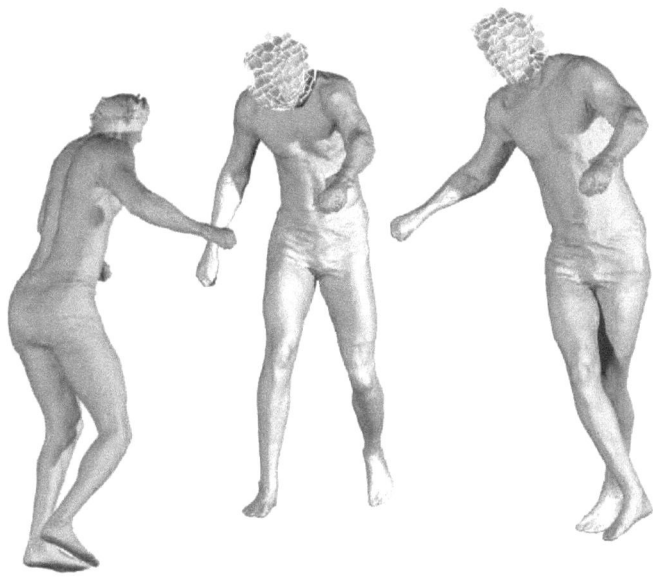

FIGURE 5.7: Animation result. The subject on the right is crossing his legs. This is significant as no subject in the database has been scanned in a similar pose.

intuitively most of the investigated properties can be approximated well, given triangle shape and local curvature information.

Similar to the muscularity application and following a current trend of face beautification papers [35, 61, 67], it would be interesting to do the same for human body shapes, *i.e.*, to create a body shape beauty evaluation system which could then be used to improve the perceived physical attractiveness of a person. Morphing a subject tracked in a video according to this deformation field would be a further interesting step.

Furthermore, a variation of the handle based deformation technique introduced in Section 5.4 can be applied to vision tasks as detailed in the next chapter. The main difference is that the constraints are extracted from vision input data rather than being specified manually.

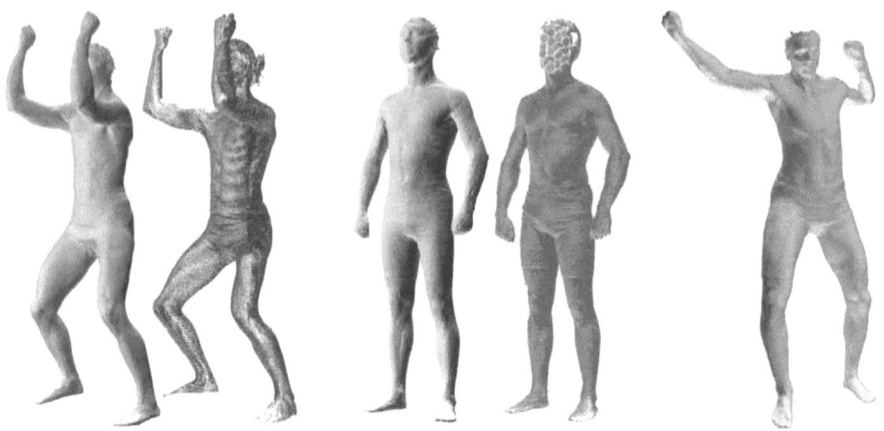

FIGURE 5.8: **left**: Morphing a scan into a pose that is not in the database in comparison with the original scan. The hands are not turned into the same direction which results in the main difference between the two. **Middle**: The scan of a person who is not in the database is projected into the space of body shapes. **Right**: The subject on the left is morphed into the spear-thrower's pose.

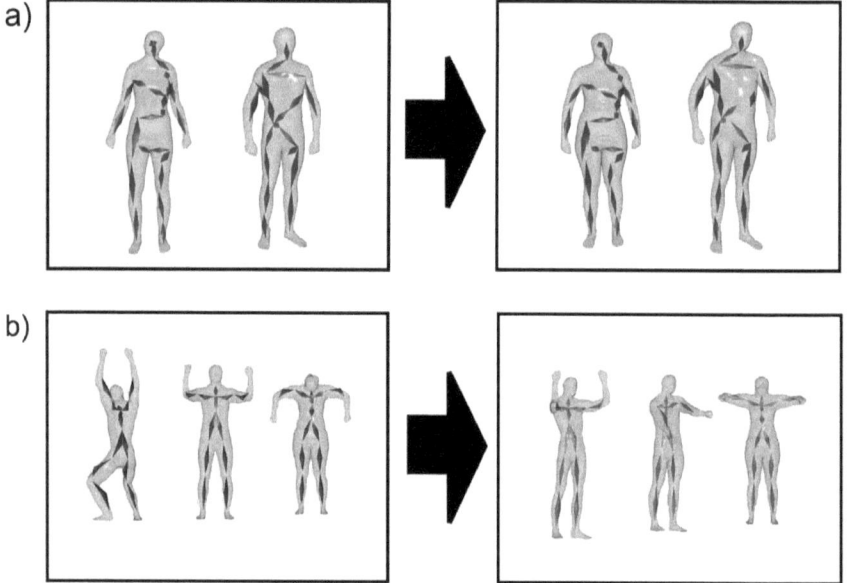

FIGURE 5.9: a) changing the shape of the human model with the extracted shape skeleton, b) changing the pose of the human model with the extracted pose skeleton.

5.7. Discussion

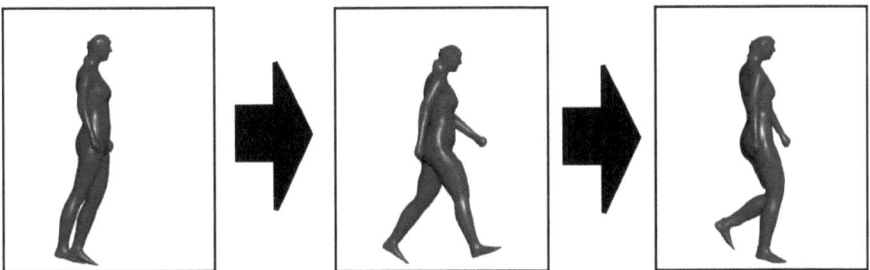

FIGURE 5.10: The extracted combined shape and pose skeleton allows independent control of shape and pose. In this example a walking motion is performed while changing the body shape.

> Du suchst ein Stück Fels mit dem
> höchsten Schwierigkeitsgrad und darin
> den Weg des geringsten Widerstandes.
> WOLFGANG GÜLLICH

Chapter 6

Estimation Applications

In contrast to the previous chapter, which showed applications focused on synthesis of shapes given semantic constraints, in this chapter estimation applications are explored. That is, given typical vision input data, the task is to estimate shape and pose of an observed person. The methods are mainly targeted at estimating shape and pose parameters from multi-view stereo images, videos, and monocular images but also from 3D scans of dressed subjects.

Since not all representations lend themselves equally well to the presented applications they have been implemented using only the most appropriate approaches. The approach in Section 6.1 assumes an exceptional position because its input data are 3D scans rather than images, which is still an uncommon input data format in today's vision community. Yet, since the advent of affordable time-of-flight depth cameras, 3D data as input has become increasingly popular. A general approach for estimating pose and shape from still images or multi-view video streams using the differential rotation encoding is presented in Section 6.2. Results for various input data generated with the approach are presented. Multiview images are analysed in Sec. 6.3, multiview markerless motion capture is performed in Sec. 6.4, and monocular pose estimation is carried out in Sec. 6.5. Section 6.6 addresses a very similar problem as Section 6.5, namely, estimating pose and shape of a subject from monocular images. Only

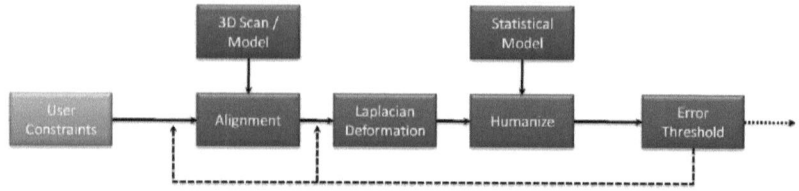

FIGURE 6.1: Overview of the fitting algorithm

the second approach generalises the setting. In addition to pose and shape estimation a rough estimate of a projective camera is made and instead of the differential rotation encoding (from Sec. 4.2) the factorisation method (from Sec. 4.3) is employed. A discussion concludes the chapter in Sec. 6.7.

6.1 Shape Estimation from Dressed 3D Scans

Fitting a human model $\mathcal{M}$ to a 3D scan or model $\mathcal{S}$ is done with an iterative approach as illustrated in Figure 6.1. We start with a sparse set of user specified correspondence points. Marking feet, hands, elbows, and head is usually sufficient. We then iterate three steps until convergence. In the first step $\mathcal{M}$ is aligned rigidly to $\mathcal{S}$ by finding the set of closest points from $\mathcal{M}$ to $\mathcal{S}$ and minimising the squared distance. Next, the matches are used to drive a least-squares Laplacian deformation, moving $\mathcal{M}$ closer to $\mathcal{S}$. As this action normally moves the model out of the space spanned by the statistical model of human bodies, we finally project $\mathcal{M}$ back into the human body shape space. In the following we describe the three main steps in more detail.

6.1.1 Alignment

For every point of $\mathcal{M}$ the closest point on $\mathcal{S}$ is computed. Matches are dropped if the distance is too big ($> 10\,\text{cm}$) or normal directions of source and target

6.1. Shape Estimation from Dressed 3D Scans

deviate too strongly (> 30°). The remaining matches are stored in a list $\mathcal{C}$. Then, the optimal rigid body motion is calculated by minimising the squared distances of the matches in $\mathcal{C}$. Then, $\mathcal{M}$ is transformed accordingly. This procedure is iterated until the mean residual error q of matches converges. The ICP procedure is necessary because the best alignment can only be computed for a given set of matches. It is possible, and in our experience quite likely, that given the configuration after a single alignment step, a better set of matches can be found because the objects are now aligned more closely.

6.1.2 Laplacian Deformation

Next, $\mathcal{M}$ is deformed using a simple linear least-squares Laplacian mesh deformation [2]. Specifically, the following energy is minimised:

$$\arg\min_{\mathbf{x}} \ (\mathbf{Lx} - \mathbf{d})^2 + (\mathbf{Cx} - \mathbf{c})^2, \tag{6.1}$$

where $\mathbf{L}$ and $\mathbf{d}$ are a Laplacian system with cotangent weights, and $\mathbf{C}$ and $\mathbf{c}$ represent the constraints $\mathcal{C}$ computed in the previous step, weighted by the importance function $W(i)$. If the person in the target scan is wearing tight fitting clothes, generating uniform weights is sufficient to produce convincing results. In case of wider and more obstructive clothes though this scheme fails. One main observation leading to an improved weighting function is that the human body always lies either exactly *on* the target surface or *beneath* it. Thus it is important to weight matches that constrain vertices, which lie on the outside (as determined by normal direction) of the target surface stronger than those which lie on the inside of the target. In case of a given segmentation of $\mathcal{S}$ computed with prior knowledge, for example the skin colour detection [24] or garment detection employing a model of the clothes as in [49], we could further modify the importance function to reflect this information.

6.1.3 Humanisation

Once the mesh has been deformed with the given constraints, it needs to be projected back into the space of human body shapes defined by one of the statistical models described in the previous chapter because we are not interested in just fitting the surface of the scan but to find the human body shape that best fits the scan. In principle this step projects the unconstrained solution back onto the solution manifold.

This is achieved by transforming the current model $\mathcal{M}$ into the relative rotation encoding $\mathbf{m}$. The model is then projected into the space of human body shapes using Equation (4.5). Since the pseudo-inverse of the matrix describing shape and pose $\mathbf{W}^+$ can be precomputed (*cf*. Eq. (4.5)), this step reduces to a matrix vector multiplication. The result of which is a closest fit of $\mathcal{M}$ in the space of human body shapes. Due to the limited dimension of the shape descriptor $\mathbf{s}$, shapes that are not human body shapes cannot be represented easily. Reconstructing $\mathcal{M}'$ from $\mathbf{s}$ using Equation (4.1) with subsequent Poisson reconstruction [116] yields the humanized model in Euclidean space.

6.1.4 Error Evaluation

Given the humanized mesh, we can calculate the mean length q' of the matches generated in the alignment step. If q' is lower than q we continue with the alignment step, otherwise the Laplacian Deformation is repeated with reduced weights for the matches. After a fixed number of iterations (10) with $q' > q$ the algorithm terminates.

As for all ICP methods, the initial configuration has to be fairly close to the solution for the approach to converge. This issue can be avoided if a few markers are placed manually on the target surface. Then, to generate the initial configuration the same algorithm is run with these fixed matches.

6.1.5 Experiments

In this section several experiments are performed to evaluate the approach. Of course, since no statistical analysis is performed, no definitive conclusions about the approach can be drawn. However, we believe that strong evidence towards general applicability of the method is presented. First, the hidden body geometry of several persons is estimated and biometric measures are extracted and compared to the true values. Then, registration bootstrapping, a technique for improving the quality of scan registration and increasing the size of the scan database, is demonstrated. Last, the same technique is applied to shape estimation from partially missing and severely noise corrupted data.

The experimental setup is conceivably simple. A full body 3D scanner is used to scan the subjects, which takes about 10 seconds. Then, using a custom tool, markers are selected (2 min). Finally, the proposed approach is run. The runtime of our Matlab implementation of the algorithm is in the order of minutes per scan. *E.g.*, for the scan shown in Figure 6.3b, marker based registration takes 3.5 min (20 iterations) and the surface registration 8 min (22 iterations).

6.1.6 Hidden Body Geometry

We evaluate our technique for estimating hidden body geometry, on the one hand, by showing overlays of the scan with the estimated geometry and on the other, by extracting biometric measures from the estimations. Overlays of resulting estimations are shown in Figure 6.3. As can be seen, the estimated body shapes are highly plausible and fit well into the overlaid 3D scans. For a scan as shown in Figure 6.4 it is extremely difficult to estimate measures such as dress size or body weight of the Santa impersonator because the thick coat generates an ambiguous situation that is even difficult for humans to resolve. However, some measures, such as the length of arms and legs and his total height, can be recovered quite well (*cf.* Table 6.1). Note that the input data

6.1. Shape Estimation from Dressed 3D Scans

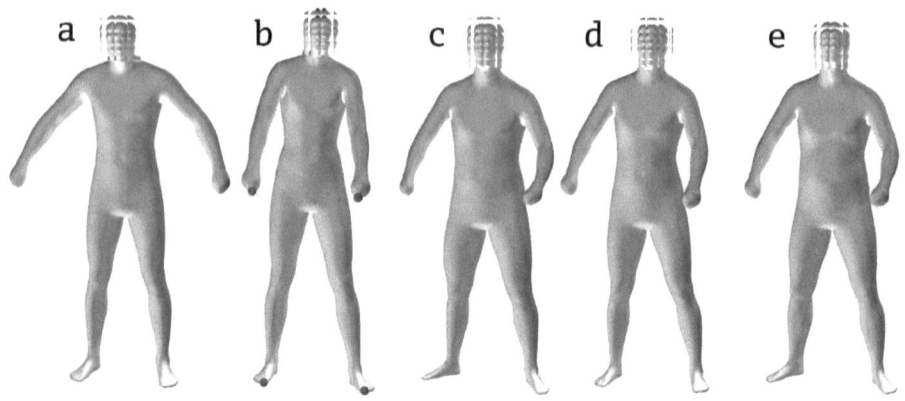

FIGURE 6.2: The optimisation procedure is based on iterative deformation of the model using Laplacian editing followed by a projection of the result onto the solution manifold spanned by the model of human body shapes. This figure shows some of the steps performed during the optimisation. In **a** the initial mesh (the average man) and in **b** the result of the marker based fitting is shown. **c** and **d** display a Laplace deformation step followed by a humanisation at different points in the optimisation. Lastly, the final humanized result is displayed in **e**.

for the algorithm does not have to be generated by a 3D scanner. Structured light scanners or multi-view stereo techniques provide sufficient 3D geometry.

The progression of the optimisation is displayed in Figure 6.2. Starting from the average man, markers are used to get an initial pose estimate. Please note that the body shape of this initial estimate (Fig. 6.2b) differs significantly from the final result (Fig. 6.2e). This indicates that the markers merely stabilise the optimisation but do not contribute considerably to the shape estimate. The initial estimate is taller, thinner and uses outstretched instead of slightly bent arms to reach the hand markers.

Estimating biometric measures given a 3D model of a human is a difficult problem. Two of the simplest and most prominent solutions include computing the measures directly on the estimated 3D model or employing the statistical model of human body shapes to learn functions that compute the desired measures. Some measures, such as weight, cannot be computed directly from a given mesh of a human. However, even for length measurements that can easily

6.1. Shape Estimation from Dressed 3D Scans

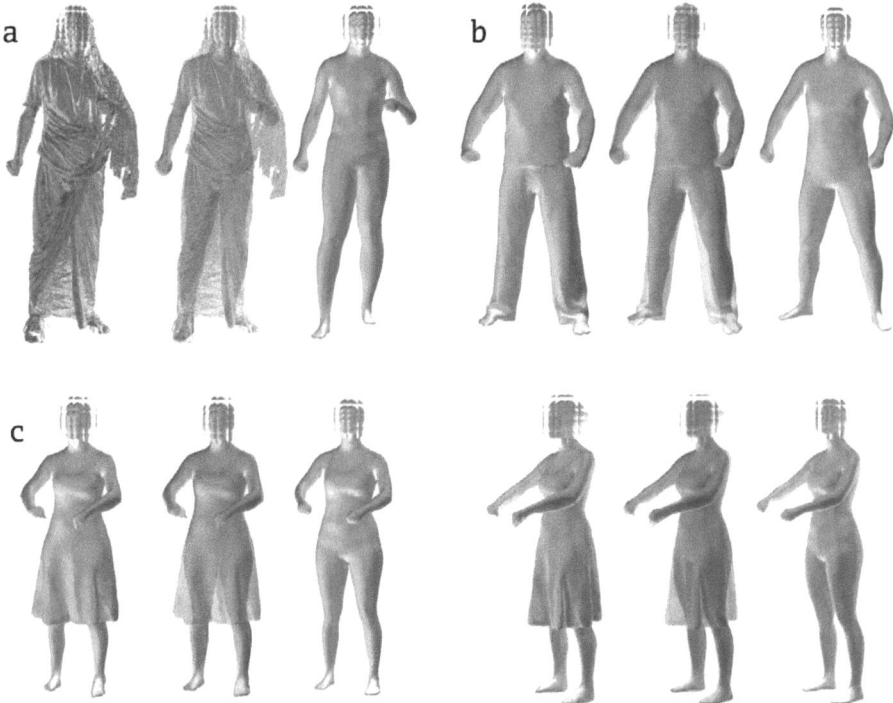

FIGURE 6.3: Body shape estimation can be performed given 3D data generated by a laser scanner (a) or by silhouette based multi camera systems (b and c).

be computed on a mesh surface, we found that fitting a filtered linear function to the statistical model achieves better results [51]. The measures summarised in Table 6.1 are consequently computed by training a linear function on the statistical human body shape model. For dressed humans, a weight factor of 10 between matches of vertices lying outside vs. inside the target surface was found to be optimal.

6.1.7 Registration Bootstrapping

Given, for example, a scan, as shown in Figure 6.5a, we apply the surface registration procedure described in [51]. First, a skeleton based pose estimation

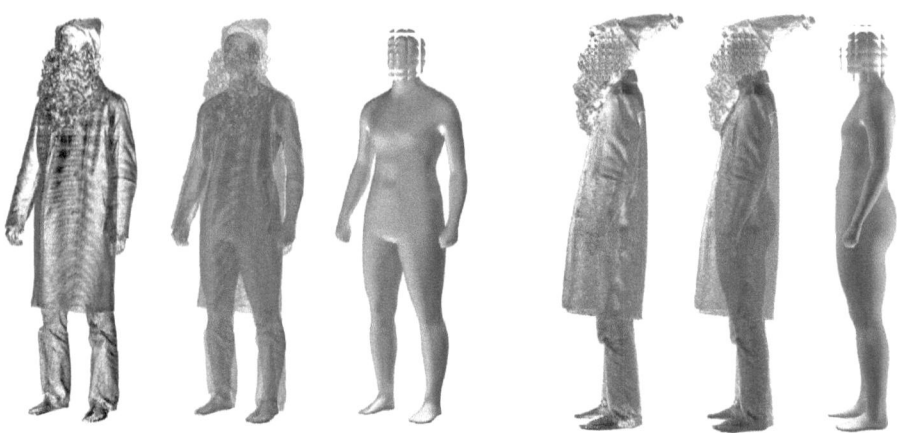

FIGURE 6.4: Even for humans, it is impossible to accurately estimate the body shape of a person wearing heavy clothing. So, the estimation of some biometric measures can only be achieved with limited accuracy. Generally, lengths, e.g. arm length or body height can still be estimated but circumference based measures (waist girth, weight, etc.) are obscured.

	Height	Arm Length	Leg Length	Weight	Waist Girth
Santa	178	61	77	76	75
full	178	60	77	71	75
partial	181	57	79	64	75
ground truth	182	57	79	63	74
Toga	175	61	80	69	73
ground truth	179	59	84	67	74

TABLE 6.1: Biometric measures of one person: First dressed as a **Santa** impersonator (Fig. 6.4), and second wearing every day clothing (Fig. 6.7) using the **full** and a **partial** scan, as well as manually acquired ground truth values for comparison. Additionally, biometric measures of the subject wearing a **toga** shown in Figure 6.12a are compared to ground truth. Lengths are measured in cm and weight in kg.

is performed (Fig. 6.5b) to generate a starting point for the subsequent non-rigid surface registration shown in Figure 6.5c. Unfortunately, due to the large difference in body shape of template and scan a registration error occurs in the left armpit. This is a result of the skeleton based initial pose estimation which does not model different body shapes. As a result, the starting configuration for the non-rigid surface registration step may be quite far away from the target surface, if the body shape is significantly different. This is not much

6.1. Shape Estimation from Dressed 3D Scans

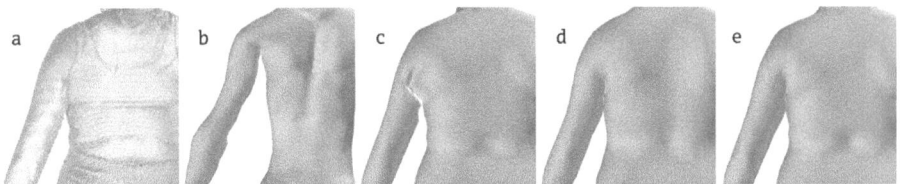

FIGURE 6.5: The quality of registration can be improved by using the statistical model to generate an improved starting point for the surface fitting step. The figure shows an input scan (a), a skeleton based initial guess (b), the surface fitting result using that initial guess (c), the initial guess generated by our system (d), and the final surface fitting result.

of a problem in smoothly varying areas, such as the chest region, but in unfortunate circumstances, the mesh can self-intersect or creases may develop. These problems can be alleviated, if a better initial guess can be generated (*cf*. Fig. 6.5d). Our approach is similar to the bootstrapping for facial scans described by Blanz *et al.* [10]. We perform the same fitting algorithm as described above for naked/tightly dressed scans with uniform constraint weights. Figure 6.5e shows the improvements when bootstrapping is applied.

This procedure can not only be applied to increase the database size but to improve the quality of scans already part of the database. In fact, the model shown in Figure 6.5 was already part of the database.

It may seem surprising, that for a model which is already in the database, the gradient descent based fitting procedure does not arrive at the exact representation of the scan. Since fitting starts from the average model and registration errors, as shown in Figure 6.5c, can be considered outliers, the gradient descent based registration technique is unable to find that specific minimum of the cost function.

An example of employing the bootstrapping procedure to a scan that is not in the database is shown in Figure 6.6. The initial guess models the scan very well already. So the surface fitting step is only required to fill in minor details instead of being responsible for performing major alignment of template and target surface.

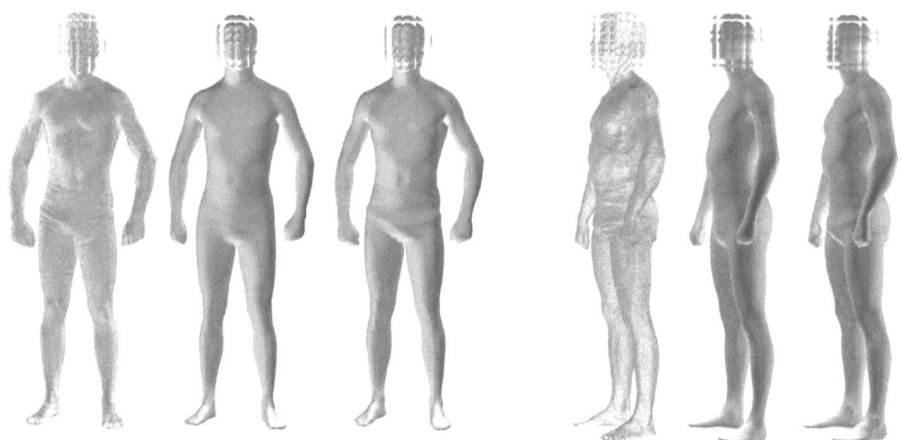

FIGURE 6.6: Using a bootstrapping technique, it is easily possible to increase the size of the scan database. Here, the input scan, the initial, model based estimate, and the final surface fit are shown. Since the initial estimate is already very close to the scan surface, a high quality semantic registration can be reached.

6.1.8 Scan Completion

In a similar vein, it is possible to estimate body shape from incomplete scans as present, for example, when structured light or range scanners are used. In Figure 6.7a a laser scan acquired from a single direction is shown. In comparison the full scan and the resulting body shapes are shown in Figure 6.7b. The two reconstructions are very similar as also evidenced in Table 6.1.

6.1.9 Noise

Robustness to noise is an important property for any algorithm working on real world input data. In Figure 6.8 Gaussian noise is added to a 3D scan. Then, the unmodified algorithm described in Figure 6.1 is run on the data. The result looks plausible and the pose is only slightly misestimated.

6.2. Pose and Body Shape Estimation

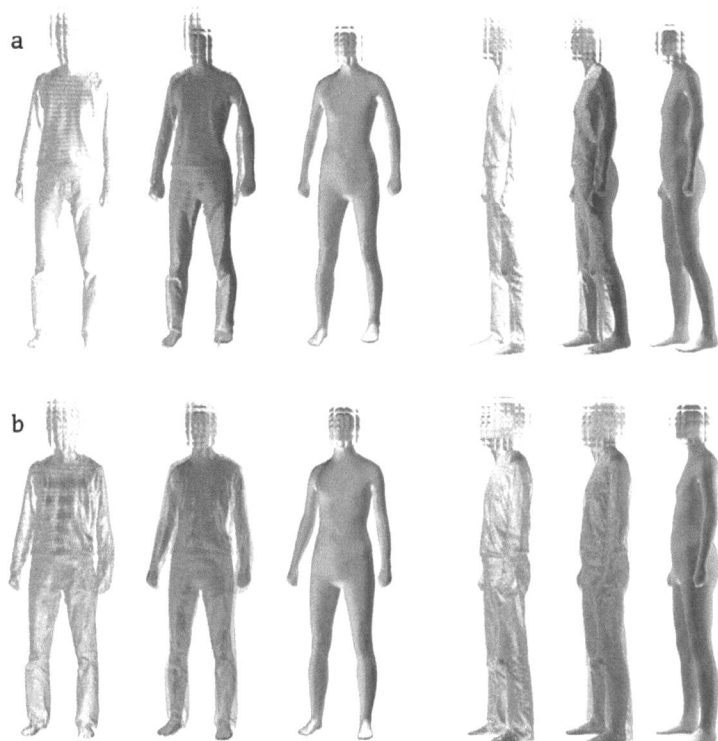

FIGURE 6.7: The model is fitted to a single view 3D scan of a subject wearing every day garments (**top**) as well as to the corresponding full multi-view 3D scan (**bottom**).

6.2 Pose and Body Shape Estimation

In this section, a similar approach is applied to the related problem of estimating human pose and body shape from still images or multi-view video streams, given a statistical shape and pose model. First, the method for finding the pose and shape in images or for initialising the first frame of a sequence is presented. Afterwards, the tracking procedure is introduced.

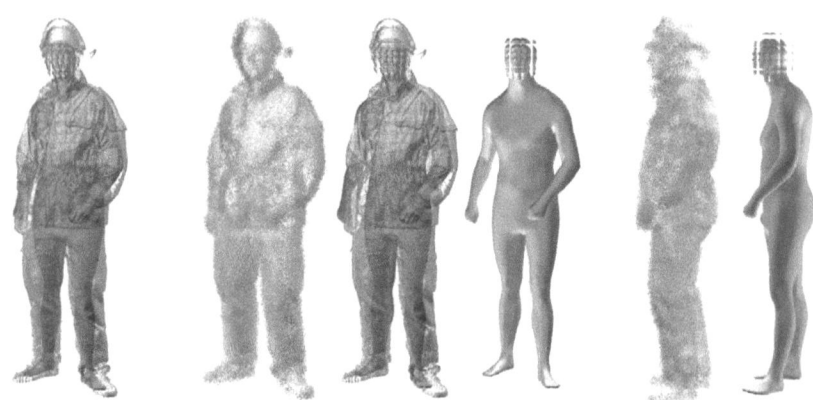

FIGURE 6.8: The approach is robust even to severe noise corruption. Here we analyse the body of a fully dressed emergency medical technician (EMT). On the left the uncorrupted scan overlaid with a model fit to that scan is shown. The rest of the figure shows the noise corrupted scan, the result overlaid with the original scan, and the result on its own.

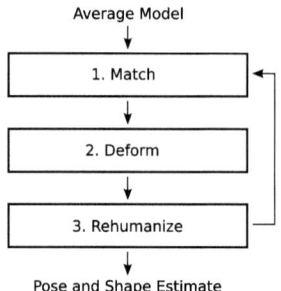

FIGURE 6.9: Steps of the optimisation procedure for silhouette based fitting. Starting from the average model, three steps are iterated until convergence is reached. First, matches between measured and rendered silhouettes are computed; second, based on these constraints, non rigid deformation of the model is performed; and third, the model is rehumanised.

6.2.1 Pose and Shape from Silhouettes

For the initialisation of pose and shape from a single image or a set of images a silhouette based ICP procedure is employed. As shown in Fig. 6.9, it comprises the three steps: match, deform, and rehumanise, which are described in the following.

6.2.1.1 Match

In this step, first the contour of the 3D model is rendered into the input frame and the silhouette of the subject is extracted from the input image. Then, closest point matches between contour and silhouette are computed. Matches are discarded, if the estimated normals do not match ($> 30^o$) or no approximate inverse matches can be found. The remaining matches are associated with vertices of the mesh.

The matches are fundamentally 2D-3D correspondences, *i.e.*, only two degrees of freedom of the 3D geometry can effectively be constrained. The depth as seen from the camera is completely unconstrained. But not even two constrained dimensions can necessarily be justified by the input data. Szelinski showed that in the context of general feature detection a feature can be located exactly, if its variance is large in both image directions [106]. In many cases, however, a silhouette can locally be approximated by a straight line. In this case the variance of a feature on this silhouette is large only in normal direction to the boundary of the silhouette.

Therefore, in contrast to existing approaches, we employ 1D-3D constraints instead of 2D-3D constraints by only considering the distance to the measured silhouette in normal direction. This allows slippage of the constraint along the contour. It can be observed that by replacing all 2D-3D correspondences with 1D-3D correspondences, the range of convergence can be increased drastically.

FIGURE 6.10: By replacing 2D-3D constraint with 1D-3D constraints performance of the gradient descent algorithm can be improved significantly. **Left**: Initialisation with the average human. **Middle**: The optimisation result using 2D-3D constraints. **Right**: The optimisation result using 1D-3D constraints.

In Figure 6.10 a comparison of 1D-3D and 2D-3D constraints is performed. For the photograph of Abraham Lincoln optimisation was performed twice comparing 1D-3D and 2D-3D constraints. Due to the large height difference between the mean human shown on the left and Lincoln's 1.93 m frame and the sticky behaviour of 2D-3D constraints, the model is not able to grow. Using 1D-3D constraints, however, solves the issue. For details about the fitting procedure for monocular still images please refer to Section 6.5.

6.2.1.2 Deform

First, the rigid body motion (RBM) with rotation matrix $\mathbf{R}$ and translation vector $\mathbf{t}$ is computed, which best fits the current mesh to the constraints. This requires solving a system of equations of the form

$$(\mathbf{R}\,\mathbf{l}_i + \mathbf{t} - \mathbf{o}_i) \cdot \mathbf{n}_i = 0, \qquad (6.2)$$

where $\mathbf{l}_i$ is the ith constrained vertex, and $\mathbf{o}_i$ and $\mathbf{n}_i$ are the corresponding constraint position in world coordinates and its normal. Afterwards, the matches are used as one dimensional constraints for a linear least-squares Laplace deformation [2]. After several iterations of these steps, a deformed mesh that fits

6.2. Pose and Body Shape Estimation

well to the data is generated. However, depending on the quality of the input silhouettes, the resulting mesh may have lost some of its human traits.

6.2.1.3 Rehumanise

To ameliorate this problem the statistical model is taken into account to maintain a plausible human shape. The aim is to fit the mesh as closely as possible to the observed silhouettes while maintaining a semblance of humanness. Here, the rotation invariant encoding proposed in Section 4.1 is employed. The database of scanned humans represents a solution manifold, which must not be left for the result to be valid. This can be enforced by projecting the resulting mesh of the Laplace deformation into the eigenspace of human shapes and poses and reconstructing a rehumanised mesh from the coefficients. Dependent on the application, the splitting in pose and shape introduced in Section 4.2 can be used to restrict the allowed deformation to pose, shape, or the full body shape and pose model.

6.2.2 Forward Tracking

After the initialisation of the first frame has been computed based on silhouettes alone, a more complex tracking procedure is used, which is, however, still based on the constrained ICP procedure proposed above.

Assuming that a good approximation of the previous frame has been computed, we can use feature tracks computed on the input video to track the mesh forward through time. The well-known KLT tracker [95] is used to compute sparse feature tracks on the input video. Ray casting is used to associate the 2D position of tracks in the first image with vertices. The target positions are used as 2D constraints. Performing a few (3) iterations of the constrained ICP procedure, leads to a good initialisation for the next frame.

6.2.3 Optical Flow Based Correction

In order to improve the fitting, additional constraints need to be generated. Optical flow is computed between a rendered model in the current pose and the current multi-view input frame. In both images the green channel is replaced with the measured and rendered silhouette, respectively, to improve fitting in areas where the texture of fore- and background are very similar. With most optical flow algorithms severe problems occur at occlusion boundaries because smoothness constraints in the flow computation create artifacts in the mesh deformation step. The flow by Ogale and Aloimonos [75], however, detects occlusion boundaries and outputs a map of occluded pixels in addition to the optical flow vectors. By masking these areas out, the problems with occlusion boundaries can be reduced. The flow constraints can be trivially converted to 2D-3D constraints, which, in turn, are applied to deforming the mesh as described above.

6.2.4 Constant Shape

Usually, if this approach is applied to a sequence of images, the body shape does not stay constant. However, since a model is available that effectively splits the solution space into shape and pose dependent subspaces, it is possible to enforce constant shape coefficients. We propose to optimise a given frame n using first the full model (shape and pose), then optimising the shape for all frames seen so far, and lastly estimating the pose for frame n given the shape. Using Equation (4.15) the optimisation of the full model can easily be done. Afterwards, the following equation is solved for the accumulated shape s_a

$$\begin{bmatrix} \mathbf{m}_1 \\ \vdots \\ \mathbf{m}_n \end{bmatrix} = \begin{bmatrix} \mathbf{S} \\ \vdots \\ \mathbf{S} \end{bmatrix} \cdot \mathbf{s}_a + \begin{bmatrix} \mathbf{P} \cdot \mathbf{p}_1 \\ \vdots \\ \mathbf{P} \cdot \mathbf{p}_n \end{bmatrix} + \begin{bmatrix} \mathbf{a} \\ \vdots \\ \mathbf{a} \end{bmatrix}, \qquad (6.3)$$

where all poses $\mathbf{p}_i$ are held constant. The least squares solution of this equation system is equivalent to computing the mean of all shape coefficients $\mathbf{s}_i$ seen so far. In the last step, the following equation is solved for $\mathbf{p}$

$$\mathbf{m} = \mathbf{P} \cdot \mathbf{p} + \mathbf{S} \cdot \mathbf{s}_a + \mathbf{a}. \tag{6.4}$$

Since all these equation systems involve constant matrices, the respective pseudoinverses can be precomputed. Thus, computing a solution involves only a single matrix vector multiplication.

6.3 Shape Estimation from Multi-View Images

In order to quantitatively estimate the method for shape estimation from images, we project 3D scans of subjects (*cf*. Figs. 6.11 and 6.12) who are not part of the scan database into a number of views. The shape estimation algorithm is run on different numbers of projections. Since the silhouette-based ICP algorithm converges to a local minimum, if the initial rotation of the mesh is significantly different from the real orientation, the algorithm is run 16 times with orientations distributed evenly around the vertical axis and the result with the smallest residual error is chosen as the final result.

Quantitative analysis of the results is performed by extracting anthropometric measures from the resulting scans using the method from [51] and comparing them to ground truth values. The results, summarised in Table 6.2 and 6.3, show that one camera is already sufficient to accurately estimate the height of a person. However, since the model was trained on tightly dressed subjects the weight of casually dressed persons is generally overestimated. For the tightly dressed subject, however, the weight can be estimated accurately.

For the tightly dressed scan (subject 4), we also compute the root mean squared distance from the estimated mesh to the scan, for one to eight projections. These distances are summarised in Table 6.4. As this error as well as the height

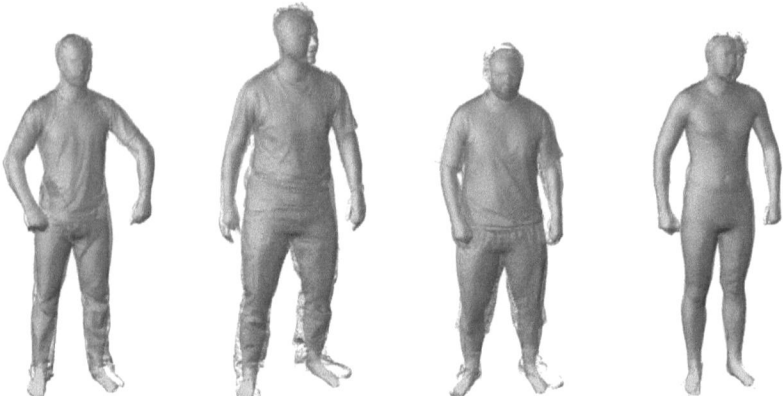

FIGURE 6.11: Four subjects, who are not in the database, are scanned with a 3D laser scanner. The scans are projected into four views and the shape estimation algorithm is run on the generated silhouettes. Here, the input scan overlaid with the resulting mesh is shown.

	estimated height using # projections								true
	1	2	3	4	5	6	7	8	
subject 1	1.75	1.76	1.75	1.75	1.75	1.76	1.76	1.76	1.76
subject 2	1.87	1.86	1.87	1.87	1.90	1.87	1.89	1.90	1.89
subject 3	1.70	1.72	1.73	1.71	1.73	1.73	1.74	1.74	1.73
subject 4	1.80	1.79	1.78	1.79	1.79	1.79	1.79	1.79	1.79

TABLE 6.2: Height estimates [m] and the true height of the four subjects shown in Fig. 6.11 using an increasing number of views. Even in the monocular case accurate results can be obtained.

	estimated weight using # projections								true
	1	2	3	4	5	6	7	8	
subject 1	70	74	80	83	83	84	85	86	73
subject 2	87	92	101	101	103	111	107	108	95
subject 3	74	83	83	92	86	91	90	95	85
subject 4	78	75	75	75	76	77	76	76	75

TABLE 6.3: Weight estimates [kg] and the true weight of the four subjects shown in Fig. 6.11 using an increasing number of views. Although the information that can be gained from a single view is limited, reasonable weight estimates can be computed even in this case.

6.3. Shape Estimation from Multi-View Images

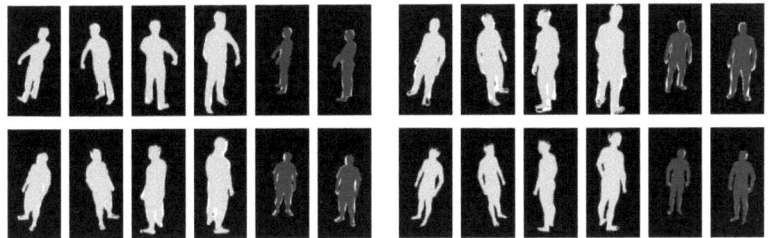

FIGURE 6.12: Four 3D scans of different subjects are projected into virtual cameras. Shape estimation is performed and the result is overlaid into the input images (yellow). The two additional images show that the estimation fits well also in views that were not used in the optimisation (blue).

number of views	1	2	3	4	5	6	7	8
RMSE [mm]	9.2	8.1	8.1	7.9	7.5	9.6	7.9	8.3

TABLE 6.4: RMSE of the estimated body shape compared to the ground truth laser scan of subject 4 using the given number of views. Evidently, the estimation error is not significantly dependent on the number of views and degrades gracefully even for the monocular case.

and weight estimates do not vary considerably, we can assume that our approach is not significantly dependent on the number of views.

We experienced that the visual quality of shape fitting can be further improved, if a gender specific starting point is used. After first performing the silhouette-based ICP procedure starting from an average model, the gender can be detected. Correct gender classification is possible for all examples considered in this paper. Then the optimisation is repeated starting from the average male/female model.

The algorithm is also tested on real images. If a calibrated set of images is available, an accurate estimate of a person can be generated. Figure 6.13 shows a woman wearing a skirt, whose shape and pose are estimated from three cameras. The resulting mesh looks realistic and fits well even to the views not used in the optimisation.

FIGURE 6.13: Estimated pose and body shape of a woman wearing a skirt. The result is overlaid into input views in yellow. The blue silhouettes are results rendered into additional views to show the accuracy of the estimation (not used in the optimisation).

6.4 Tracking and Shape Stability

Starting from an initial pose and shape estimate, tracking is performed on calibrated multi-camera image sequences. Silhouettes are extracted using background subtraction. The estimation results are shown in Figure 6.16. For the HumanEva scene the precision (percentage of the estimated silhouette that overlaps the true foreground) is 95.7% and the recall (percentage of the true foreground that overlaps the estimated silhouette) is 79.0%. We also submitted the results of the HumanEva sequence to obtain a ground-truth evaluation. Our method achieves a RMSE of 37.8 mm at a std. dev. of 9.6 mm for the tracked sequence, which is comparable to other publications in the area (*cf.* [37]). A plot of the mean error over time is shown in Figure 6.14.

Figure 6.15 shows that height and weight of the estimated models remain constant during the tracking. This indicates that the proposed separation of shape and pose works effectively. Although, even the standard deviation of the optimisation without enforcing shape constancy is low, constant shape constraints help to stabilise the estimated shape.

6.6. Uncalibrated Monocular Pose Estimation

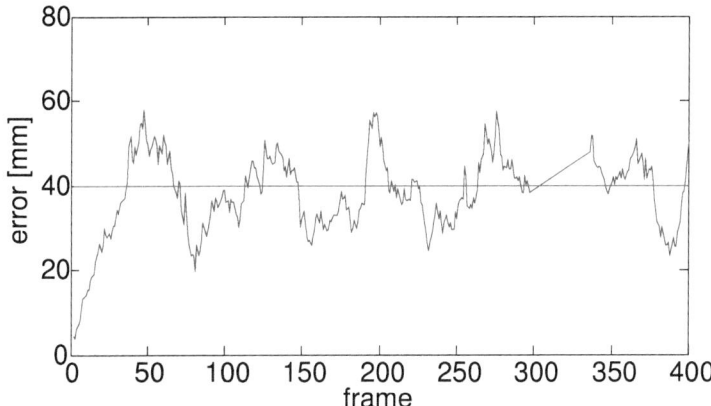

FIGURE 6.14: The per frame error as reported by the HumanEva-II evaluation compared to ground truth. The mean error and corresponding standard deviation are (37.8, std. dev. 9.6) mm.

6.5 Estimating Pose and Shape from Photographs

The approach can also be used for pose and shape estimation of persons in photographs if the silhouette of the person and a projection matrix are given. Figure 6.17 and 6.18 show four examples of shapes fitted to photographs. As with many systems, extracting foot orientation is problematic but body shape and general pose are recovered well.

6.6 Uncalibrated Monocular Pose Estimation

Similar to the approach used in the previous section, in this section pose and shape are estimated from single images. There are two main differences. Firstly, instead of using the differential rotation encoding used in the previous section, the factorisation based model introduced in Section 4.3 is applied. Secondly, in the previous section an orthographic camera model is estimated manually. Here, the orthographic camera is used only to bootstrap the optimisation. Later, the

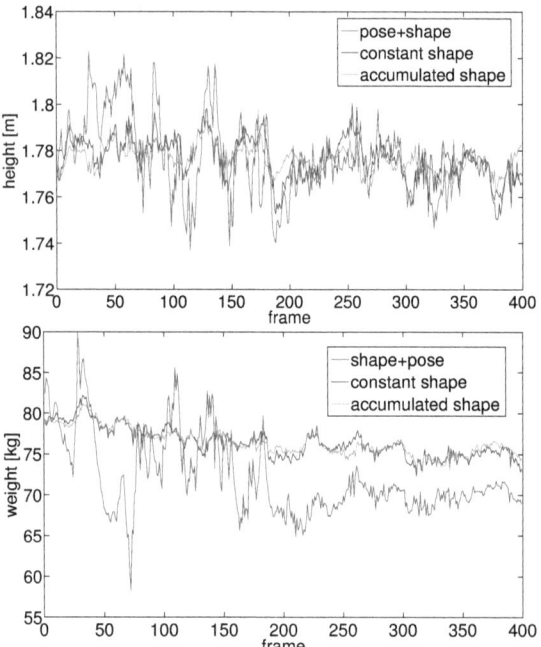

FIGURE 6.15: Three different methods for estimating shape are compared. In the first method (pose+shape) the full model including parameters for pose and shape are optimised during the rehumanisation step, *i.e.*, the constant shape enforcement (Sec. 6.2.4) is not used (std. dev. 1.65 cm and 4.7 kg). In the second and third method (constant and accumulated shape) constant shape is enforced. The second method (constant shape) estimates the anthropometric measures (std. dev. 0.93 cm and 1.8 kg) from the final mesh (**m** in Equation (6.4)) while the third method (accumulated shape) uses the accumulated shape of Equation (6.3) (std. dev. 0.59 cm and 1.6 kg).

parameters of a projective camera are optimised to improve the shape estimation. The main idea used here is that the 3D shape of the subject can be estimated accurately enough given the orthographic projection for using it as a calibration object.

6.6.1 Virtual Object Calibration

Having established 2D-3D correspondences between the silhouette and the estimated 3D shape, we can use the 3D shape as "virtual calibration object".

6.6. Uncalibrated Monocular Pose Estimation

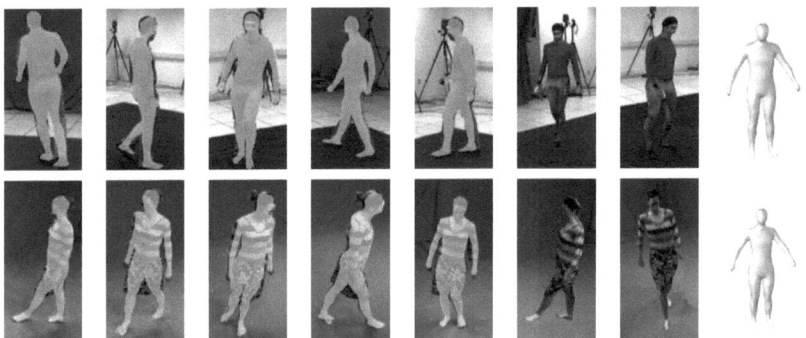

FIGURE 6.16: The markerless tracking procedure is applied to two four-camera sequences with one male and one female subject. The first sequence is taken from the HumanEva-II dataset [96], which is captured in a cluttered lab environment, whereas the second sequence is captured in a green-room. **Left to right**: Estimation results are superimposed on input frames for five views. The next two images show textured result meshes, which are used in the optical flow based correction. The last image shows the estimated shape of the subjects.

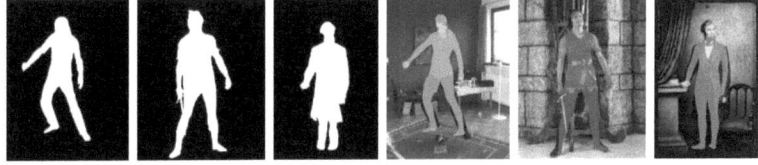

FIGURE 6.17: Pose and body shape of three subjects are estimated from a single view (an artist, Douglas Fairbanks as Robin Hood, Abraham Lincoln). Note that although the silhouette under Robin Hood's right arm is segmented badly, the fit in this area is almost perfect. For Abraham Lincoln, who reportedly was 1.93 m at 82 kg, our estimated mesh stands 1.89 m tall and weighs 82 kg.

Generally, the calibration of a perspective camera, *i.e.* determining its projection matrix and decomposing it into intrinsic and extrinsic parameters, can be performed by means of direct linear transformation once some 3D points of an observed object are known. This implies that we can use the estimated 3D shape as virtual calibration object since its 2D-3D correspondences are all known.

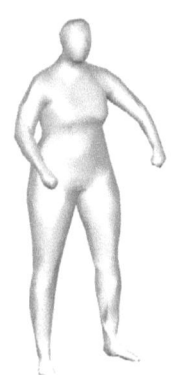

FIGURE 6.18: We also match shape and pose of this statue by Gaston Lachaise. Although the body shape cannot be recovered exactly as the statue has an unrealistically thin waist, a similar female shape is generated.

Since the projection ray of any 3D point $\mathbf{X}$ must be orthogonal to its 2D correspondence $\mathbf{x} = [x\ y\ 1]^\top$ [46], we obtain

$$\mathbf{x} \times \mathbf{PX} = 0 \qquad (6.5)$$

where $\mathbf{P}$ is the projection matrix of the perspective camera, and $\times$ denotes the cross product. This induces a linear equation system we solve for the unknown camera matrix $\mathbf{P}$.

Let $\mathbf{K}$ be the 3×3 upper-diagonal matrix of the intrinsic parameters, $\mathbf{R}$ the 3×3 matrix indicating the orientation of the camera, and $\mathbf{t}$ a 3-vector of the translation of the camera from the origin. Since

$$\mathbf{P} = \mathbf{K}\,[\mathbf{R}|\mathbf{t}], \qquad (6.6)$$

we can determine $\mathbf{K}$ and $\mathbf{R}$ from the first three columns of $\mathbf{P}$ using the fact that $\mathbf{R}$ is a rotation matrix and $\mathbf{K}$ upper-triangular by using Givens rotations [46].

6.6. Uncalibrated Monocular Pose Estimation

FIGURE 6.19: Estimation computed with an orthographic (**left**) and a projective camera (**right**).

FIGURE 6.20: **Leftmost three images**: input silhouette, result with an orthographic (middle) and a projective camera (right). **Rightmost two images**: silhouette with simulated occlusion (from hips downwards) and estimation result.

6.6.2 Camera Estimation

In Fig. 6.19 a subject is shown jumping to a climbing hold. The two images correspond to two states of the optimisation procedure. For the left image, shape is estimated using an initial orthographic camera. For the right image, a projective camera was estimated, which optimally fits the shape to the silhouette as explained in Sec. 6.6.1. Especially the parts of the subject that are most affected by perspective distortion, namely the feet, fit much better to the silhouette.

A similar result is shown in Fig. 6.20. The left three images show the same experiment as above. The model is fitted to the silhouette and results are shown before and after camera estimation. Again, the perspective correction improves the result significantly. The right two images correspond to an experiment where a partially visible silhouette was simulated by occluding the silhouette from the hips downwards. The estimated 3D shape fits well to the visible silhouette, and the legs are estimated to have a matching size. In the following, only the results after camera estimation are shown.

6.6.3 Automatic Segmentation

In many of our examples, unchecked lighting and low image quality make manual segmentation of the input essential. In some cases, however, if the background is sufficiently different from the subject, we are able to perform automatic segmentation. The example in Fig. 6.21 shows such a case. The model is first fitted to four markers on the hands and feet of the subject. This first initialisation does not fit the pose very well but it is sufficient to initialise the GrabCut segmentation algorithm [84]. The resulting silhouette is accurate in most parts. Only between the legs the trees are wrongly classified as foreground. This is the reason that the left foot of the snowboarder is estimated to be too high. Repeating the procedure with a better starting point resolves the segmentation issue, and the computed 3D shape finally fits the silhouette well.

6.6.4 Paintings

One difficulty with paintings is that the artist may have chosen to deform the subjects. For instance, in the painting in Fig. 6.22 (*Hay Harvest at Éragny* by Camille Pissarro) the women have unrealistically long arms. The effect on pose estimation is that the fit seems to be of low quality at first glance but since the learned shape model forbids unrealistic human shapes, the computed mesh adheres to regular human proportions. For the image shown in Fig. 6.23 (Rembrandt's *Night Watch*), the main difficulty during estimation of the subjects lies

6.6. Uncalibrated Monocular Pose Estimation

FIGURE 6.21: Automatic foreground segmentation. **Top row** (from left to right): Initial estimate using four markers, input to GrabCut, output of GrabCut, and estimation result. **Bottom row**: Second iteration of the approach. GrabCut input, GrabCut output, and result are shown.

FIGURE 6.22: The women in the painting *Hay Harvest at Éragny* by Camille Pissarro have exceptionally long arms. This cannot be explained by the model. The learned shape model enforces a fit that strictly adheres to common human proportions.

in the irregular silhouettes. The militiamen wear hats, carry guns and swords. Still, a good approximation of the characters can be computed.

6.6.5 Multiple Images

The previous examples showed pose and shape estimates computed from a single image. If, however, several images of one subject are available an improved shape estimate can be computed by considering all available information. This

FIGURE 6.23: The poses of three subjects from Rembrandt's *Night Watch* are estimated. The difficulty here is that the silhouettes are highly irregular.

is demonstrated in Fig. 6.24. It shows the input silhouettes (left image of each row), estimation results by independently fitting a 3D shape to each image (second column), and the results after enforcing that shape coefficients are equal for all input images (third column). The figure also shows side-by-side comparisons of the estimated 3D shapes in the observed poses (right column).

6.7 Discussion

In this chapter, diverse vision applications that benefit from the availability of a shape and pose model are presented. In principle, all approaches presented in this chapter are variations on three steps: Constraint computation, Deformation, and Humanisation. Only the implementation details vary.

- Constraint computation is performed differently depending primarily on the type of input data. For images and 3D scans closest points from the current solution to the data are computed. For videos, additionally, feature tracks and optical flow are computed to add constraints to the inside of the measured silhouettes.

6.7. Discussion

FIGURE 6.24: If multiple views one subject are available conjoint optimisation improves the stability of the estimation. Three columns (**left to right**) input silhouette, estimate with variable shape, result after jointly optimising shape. The fourth column shows the estimated shapes before and after optimisation with constant shape.

- Deformation is always performed using a type of Laplacian deformation. Yet, using this method is not critical. Other deformation methods that result in smooth surfaces could be used.

- Humanisation is achieved by projecting the deformed mesh into the space of shapes and poses the particular model spans. This involves encoding it in a specific way, solving a linear equation system (the projection), which can be preinverted, and the generation of the final mesh. Depending on the used model, this step can be computationally expensive.

This procedure basically solves a constrained optimisation problem in a gradient descent fashion. The three steps map to the following actions: Constraint computation defines a gradient, Deformation performs a step in this direction and Humanisation projects the proposed solution back onto the solution manifold.

Interestingly, the convergence of the algorithm is better when the factorisation model is used than for the other two models, which exhibit about the same convergence behaviour. The reason for this behaviour can be discovered by considering the following scenario. Assume that in a tracked video sequence a subjects bends his arm from one frame to the next and only three constraints are observed on the arm: one at the hand, one at the elbow, and one at the shoulder. Laplacian deformation distributes the deformation equally over the whole arm, resulting in an arc. So the angle between all triangles along the length of the arm is approximately the same. The shape and pose model, however, 'knows' that significant bending is only allowed in the elbow region. The humanised version when using the relative rotation encoding consequently straightens out the rigid limbs and exhibits only weak bending of the elbow region. The factorisation model, on the other hand, uses absolute rotations rather than relative ones. During humanisation, the model tries to match the absolute rotations of all triangles. Thus, a much better fit can be generated in a single step.

Three of the four models introduced in Chapter 4 are employed in this chapter. Only the skeleton based model is not applied to any of the targetted vision applications because in this representation the humanisation step used in all variations of the fitting procedure cannot be implemented directly. However, using this model would be possible if principal component analysis would be performed on the parameters of the shape bones. Humanisation can then be performed by projecting onto the PCA basis of these parameters as done with the other models.

Chapter 7

> Still round the corner there may wait
> A new road or a secret gate,
> And though we pass them by today,
> Tomorrow we may come this way
> And take the hidden paths that run
> Towards the Moon or to the Sun.
>
> *The Lord of the Rings*
> J. R. R. Tolkien

Conclusion and Future Work

In this thesis an encompassing procedure for developing general models of human pose and shape is presented. The approach is based on the statistical analysis of a database of 3D scans of humans. The design and realisation of the database, aimed at covering the space of human shapes and poses, is described. The comprehensive coverage of pose and shape variations allows creating general models for synthesising human 3D models in arbitrary poses and with any human shape.

The availability of such a model is essential for many task in today's media industry. In feature film productions or video games human crowds are routinely deployed. Such a crowd can easily be created given one of the models proposed in this thesis. Similarly, in action oriented motion pictures virtual doubles are employed to perform stunts, too difficult or too dangerous to perform by real humans. In the motion picture industry quality requirements for the achieved result are exceptionally high, whereas for a customised game character the speed of animation is more important. As shown, both ends of this application spectrum in the field of animation are covered by two of the models proposed here. High quality synthesis is possible with the model based on a differential rotation encoding and real-time animation is explicitly addressed by the approach for learning linear blend skinning skeletons.

The other two models proposed in this thesis are aimed at vision tasks. Markerless human motion capture can benefit greatly from a model of shape and pose because normally a 3D model of the tracked person must be available. This requirement can be circumvented given a model of human pose and shape as the generic human shape can be adjusted to match the shape of the subject during tracking. This greatly simplifies the experimental setup in real world applications, *e.g.*, in biomedicine or sports science.

Finally, the two methods targeted at vision problems are applied to pose and shape estimation from single images. This very challenging problem is solved either fully automatically for upright standing poses or using a few manually placed markers for any pose. This application not only shows that the used pose and shape models are general enough to represent arbitrary human shapes in complex poses but that the proposed iterative constrained optimisation procedure converges well, even from significantly different start poses.

The state of the art has been expanded on in several directions. The proposed high quality model is the first model of human pose and shape that captures correlations between shape and pose. The modified version of this model, which allows controlling pose and shape independently is shown to perform competitively on the markerless motion capture benchmark HumanEva II even without using the supplied 3D shape of the tracked subject. The factorisation based method, is applied to the difficult monocular pose and shape estimation problem, which is solved competitively. Finally, the method for computing a linear blend skinning skeleton from example 3D scans is able to model not just the pose of a subject but also shape while retaining independent control of the two. This is not possible with previous methods.

Chapter 7 Conclusion and Future Work 119

As illustrated, the introduced models of human pose and shape are powerful tools with applications in diverse areas ranging from character synthesis given semantic constraints and animation to intricate vision tasks.

Except for the initial model, relative rotation encoding, none of the models introduced here captures correlations between pose and shape. For these methods the generated muscle bulging is identical independent of the base muscularity of the person, *i.e.*, when a very muscled person flexes the arm the bulging is the same as for a slim subject. This is not a problem for vision applications as the quality of the estimation that can be achieved given uncontrolled input images is too limited to make a difference but reintroducing correlations between pose and shape is beneficial for animation purposes. For the factorisation based model this could be achieved by assuming a trilinear relationship instead of the bilinear model assumed here. For the differential rotation encoding, a linear model computed on the residual errors of the described model would lead to a similar result.

As pose and shape estimation could be shown to converge well on single images, it should be possible to extend the procedure to monocular pose tracking. Pose and depth ambiguities would have to be handled by enforcing temporal consistency, but similar to the presented tracking approach (Sec. 6.3), shape could be estimated taking a whole sequence into account while pose is estimated for every frame.

Markerless human motion capture is possibly the most valuable application, for which an approach is presented in this thesis. The presented results are generally applicable but in combination with the method for markerless motion capture with unsynchronised moving cameras by Hasler *et al.* [50] the experimental setup could be simplified even further. Such a system would require only four handheld camera streams and an initial pose estimate. No 3D scan of the subject, no trigger based synchronisation, no explicit calibration of the cameras, and no foreground/background segmentation would be necessary any longer.

Bibliography

[1] ALEXA, M. Local control for mesh morphing. In *International Conference on Shape Modeling and Applications* (Los Alamitos, CA, USA, May 2001), IEEE Computer Society, pp. 209–215.

[2] ALEXA, M. Differential coordinates for local mesh morphing and deformation. *The Visual Computer 19*, 2–3 (May 2003), 105–114.

[3] ALLEN, B., CURLESS, B., AND POPOVIĆ, Z. The space of human body shapes: reconstruction and parameterization from range scans. *ACM Transactions on Graphics 22*, 3 (2003), 587–594.

[4] ALLEN, B., CURLESS, B., POPOVIĆ, Z., AND HERTZMANN, A. Learning a correlated model of identity and pose-dependent body shape variation for real-time synthesis. In *Proc. Symposium on Computer Animation* (2006), pp. 147–156.

[5] AMBERG, B., ROMDHANI, S., AND VETTER, T. Optimal step nonrigid icp algorithms for surface registration. *IEEE Conference on Computer Vision and Pattern Recognition* (June 2007), 1–8.

[6] ANGUELOV, D., SRINIVASAN, P., KOLLER, D., THRUN, S., RODGERS, J., AND DAVIS, J. Scape: shape completion and animation of people. *ACM Transactions on Graphics 24*, 3 (2005), 408–416.

[7] AZOUZ, Z. B., SHU, C., LEPAGE, R., AND RIOUX, M. Extracting main modes of human body shape variation from 3-d anthropometric

data. In *3D Digital Imaging and Modeling, International Conference on* (Los Alamitos, CA, USA, 2005), IEEE Computer Society, pp. 335–342.

[8] BARAN, I., AND POPOVIĆ, J. Automatic rigging and animation of 3d characters. *ACM Transactions on Graphics 26*, 3 (2007), 72.

[9] BINNIG, G., QUATE, C. F., AND GERBER, C. Atomic force microscope. *Phys. Rev. Lett. 56*, 9 (Mar 1986), 930–933.

[10] BLANZ, V., AND VETTER, T. A morphable model for the synthesis of 3d faces. In *ACM SIGGRAPH Papers* (New York, NY, USA, 1999), ACM Press, pp. 187–194.

[11] BOKELOH, M., BERNER, A., WAND, M., SEIDEL, H.-P., AND SCHILLING, A. Symmetry detection using line features. *Computer Graphics Forum (Proc. Eurographics 09) 28* (2009), 0–0. to appear.

[12] BOSCH, J. A., Ed. *Coordinate Measuring Machines and Systems*, 1 ed. Marcel Dekker Inc, 1995.

[13] BOTSCH, M., PAULY, M., GROSS, M., AND KOBBELT, L. Primo: coupled prisms for intuitive surface modeling. In *SGP '06: Proceedings of the fourth Eurographics symposium on Geometry processing* (Aire-la-Ville, Switzerland, Switzerland, 2006), Eurographics Association, pp. 11–20.

[14] BOTSCH, M., PAULY, M., WICKE, M., AND GROSS, M. Adaptive space deformations based on rigid cells. *Computer Graphics Forum 26*, 3 (2007), 339–347.

[15] BOTSCH, M., AND SORKINE, O. On linear variational surface deformation methods. *IEEE Transactions on Visualization and Computer Graphics 14*, 1 (2008), 213–230.

[16] BOTSCH, M., SUMNER, R., PAULY, M., AND GROSS, M. Deformation transfer for detail-preserving surface editing. In *Proceedings of Vision, Modeling, and Visualization (VMV)* (Aachen, Germany, Nov. 2006), pp. 357–364.

[17] BREGLER, C., AND MALIK, J. Tracking people with twists and exponential maps. In *IEEE Conference on Computer Vision and Pattern Recognition* (Washington, DC, USA, 1998), IEEE Computer Society, p. 8.

[18] BREGLER, C., MALIK, J., AND PULLEN, K. Twist based acquisition and tracking of animal and human kinematics. *International Journal of Computer Vision 56*, 3 (2004), 179–194.

[19] BROX, T., ROSENHAHN, B., CREMERS, D., AND SEIDEL, H.-P. High accuracy optical flow serves 3-d pose tracking: Exploiting contour and flow based constraints. In *Proc. ECCV* (Berlin, 2006), A. Leonarids, H. Bishof, and A. Prinz, Eds., vol. 3952/2006, Springer-Verlag, pp. 98–111.

[20] BROX, T., ROSENHAHN, B., AND WEICKERT, J. Three-dimensional shape knowledge for joint image segmentation and pose estimation. In *Pattern Recognition (Proc. DAGM)* (Vienna, Austria, Aug. 2005), W. Kropatsch, R. Sablatnig, and A. Hanbury, Eds., vol. 3663 of *LNCS*, Springer-Verlag, pp. 109–116.

[21] BĂLAN, A., BLACK, M., HAUSSECKER, H., AND SIGAL, L. Shining a light on human pose: On shadows, shading and the estimation of pose and shape. In *Proc. ICCV* (Oct. 2007), pp. 1–8.

[22] BĂLAN, A., SIGAL, L., BLACK, M., DAVIS, J., AND HAUSSECKER, H. Detailed human shape and pose from images. In *IEEE Conference on Computer Vision and Pattern Recognition* (June 2007), pp. 1–8.

[23] BĂLAN, A. O., AND BLACK, M. J. An adaptive appearance model approach for model-based articulated object tracking. In *IEEE Conference*

on Computer Vision and Pattern Recognition (Washington, DC, USA, 2006), IEEE Computer Society, pp. 758–765.

[24] BĂLAN, A. O., AND BLACK, M. J. The naked truth: Estimating body shape under clothing. In *Proc. ECCV* (Oct. 2008), vol. 5303, pp. 15–29.

[25] CARMO, M. D. *Differential Geometry of Curves and Surfaces.* Prentice Hall, Feb. 1976.

[26] COQUILLART, S. Extended free-form deformation: a sculpturing tool for 3d geometric modeling. In *SIGGRAPH '90: Proceedings of the 17th annual conference on Computer graphics and interactive techniques* (New York, NY, USA, 1990), ACM Press, pp. 187–196.

[27] DE AGUIAR, E., STOLL, C., THEOBALT, C., AHMED, N., SEIDEL, H.-P., AND THRUN, S. Performance capture from sparse multi-view video. *ACM Transactions on Graphics 27,* 3 (2008).

[28] DE AGUIAR, E., THEOBALT, C., MAGNOR, M., AND SEIDEL, H.-P. Reconstructing human shape and motion from multi-view video. In *Visual Media Production, 2005. CVMP 2005. The 2nd IEE European Conference on* (Nov. 2005), pp. 44–51.

[29] DE AGUIAR, E., THEOBALT, C., STOLL, C., AND SEIDEL, H.-P. Marker-less deformable mesh tracking for human shape and motion capture. In *IEEE Conference on Computer Vision and Pattern Recognition* (June 2007), pp. 1–8.

[30] DE AGUIAR, E., THEOBALT, C., THRUN, S., AND SEIDEL, H.-P. Automatic Conversion of Mesh Animations into Skeleton-based Animations. *Computer Graphics Forum (Proc. Eurographics EG'08) 27,* 2 (4 2008), 389–397.

[31] DER, K. G., SUMNER, R. W., AND POPOVIĆ, J. Inverse kinematics for reduced deformable models. *ACM Transactions on Graphics 25,* 3 (2006), 1174–1179.

[32] DEUTSCHER, J., AND REID, I. Articulated body motion capture by stochastic search. *International Journal of Computer Vision 61*, 2 (2005), 185–205.

[33] DONG, F., CLAPWORTHY, G. J., KROKOS, M. A., AND YAO, J. An anatomy-based approach to human muscle modeling and deformation. *IEEE Trans. on Vis. and Comp. Graphics 8*, 2 (2002), 154–170.

[34] DUDA, R. O., HART, P. E., AND STORK, D. G. *Pattern Classification (2nd Edition)*. Wiley-Interscience, 2000.

[35] EISENTHAL, Y., DROR, G., AND RUPPIN, E. Facial attractiveness: Beauty and the machine. *Neural Computation 18*, 1 (Jan. 2006), 119–142.

[36] FLOATER, M. S. Mean value coordinates. *Comput. Aided Geom. Des. 20*, 1 (2003), 19–27.

[37] GALL, J., ROSENHAHN, B., BROX, T., AND SEIDEL, H.-P. Optimization and filtering for human motion capture. *International Journal of Computer Vision* (Nov. 2008).

[38] GALL, J., ROSENHAHN, B., AND SEIDEL, H.-P. Drift-free tracking of rigid and articulated objects. In *IEEE Conference on Computer Vision and Pattern Recognition* (June 2008), pp. 1–8.

[39] GALL, J., STOLL, C., DE AGUIAR, E., THEOBALT, C., ROSENHAHN, B., AND SEIDEL, H.-P. Motion capture using joint skeleton tracking and surface estimation. *IEEE Conference on Computer Vision and Pattern Recognition 0* (2009), 1746–1753.

[40] GAVRILA, D. M., AND DAVIS, L. S. 3-d model-based tracking of humans in action: a multi-view approach. In *IEEE Conference on Computer Vision and Pattern Recognition* (Washington, DC, USA, 1996), IEEE Computer Society, p. 73.

[41] GELFAND, N., AND GUIBAS, L. J. Shape segmentation using local slippage analysis. In *SGP '04: Proceedings of the 2004 Eurographics/ACM SIGGRAPH symposium on Geometry processing* (New York, NY, USA, 2004), ACM, pp. 214–223.

[42] GOESELE, M., SNAVELY, N., CURLESS, B., HOPPE, H., AND SEITZ, S. Multi-view stereo for community photo collections. In *Computer Vision, 2007. ICCV 2007. IEEE 11th International Conference on* (Oct. 2007), pp. 1–8.

[43] GOLUB, G. H., AND VAN LOAN, C. F. *Matrix Computations (Johns Hopkins Studies in Mathematical Sciences)*. The Johns Hopkins University Press, Oct. 1996.

[44] GUAN, P., WEISS, A., BĂLAN, A. O., AND BLACK, M. J. Estimating human shape and pose from a single image. In *Proc. ICCV* (Kyoto, Japan, Sept. 2009).

[45] HARARY, F. *Graph Theory*. Addison-Wesley, 1994.

[46] HARTLEY, R., AND ZISSERMAN, A. *Multiple View Geometry in Computer Vision*, second ed. Cambridge University Press, 2004.

[47] HASLER, N. http://www.mpi-inf.mpg.de/resources/scandb/, Dec. 2008.

[48] HASLER, N., ACKERMANN, H., ROSENHAHN, B., THORMÄHLEN, T., AND SEIDEL, H.-P. Multilinear pose and body shape estimation of dressed subjects from image sets. In *IEEE Conference on Computer Vision and Pattern Recognition* (June 2010).

[49] HASLER, N., ROSENHAHN, B., AND SEIDEL, H.-P. Reverse engineering garments. In *Mirage* (Rocquencourt, France, Mar. 2007), A. Gagalowicz and W. Philips, Eds., Springer-Verlag, pp. 200–211.

[50] HASLER, N., ROSENHAHN, B., THORMÄHLEN, T., WAND, M., GALL, J., AND SEIDEL, H.-P. Markerless motion capture with unsynchronized moving cameras. In *IEEE Conference on Computer Vision and Pattern Recognition* (Miami, USA, June 2009), IEEE Computer Society, pp. 224–231.

[51] HASLER, N., STOLL, C., SUNKEL, M., ROSENHAHN, B., AND SEIDEL, H.-P. A statistical model of human pose and body shape. *Eurographics 28*, 2 (Mar. 2009).

[52] HASLER, N., THORMÄHLEN, T., ROSENHAHN, B., AND SEIDEL, H.-P. Learning skeletons for shape and pose. In *ACM SIGGRAPH Symposium on Interactive 3D Graphics and Games (I3D 2010)* (Washington DC, USA, Feb. 2010), pp. 23–30.

[53] HIGHAM, N. J. Computing the polar decomposition—with applications. *SIAM Journal of Scientific and Statistical Computing 7*, 4 (1986), 1160–1174.

[54] HILTON, A., BERESFORD, D., GENTILS, T., SMITH, R., AND SUN, W. Virtual people: Capturing human models to populate virtual worlds. In *CA '99: Proceedings of the Computer Animation* (Washington, DC, USA, 1999), IEEE Computer Society, p. 174.

[55] HOGG, D. Model-based vision: a program to see a walking person. *Image and Vision Computing 1*, 1 (Feb. 1983), 5–20.

[56] JALKIO, J. A., KIM, R. C., AND CASE, S. K. Three dimensional inspection using multistripe structured light. *Optical Engineering 24* (Dec. 1985), 966–974.

[57] KIRCHER, S., AND GARLAND, M. Free-form motion processing. *ACM Transactions on Graphics 27*, 2 (2008), 1–13.

[58] KOBBELT, L., CAMPAGNA, S., VORSATZ, J., AND SEIDEL, H.-P. Interactive multi-resolution modeling on arbitrary meshes. In *ACM SIGGRAPH Papers* (New York, NY, USA, 1998), ACM Press, pp. 105–114.

[59] KRUSKAL, J. B. On the shortest spanning subtree of a graph and the traveling salesman problem. *Proceedings of the American Mathematical Society 7*, 1 (Feb. 1956), 48–50.

[60] LEE, A., MORETON, H., AND HOPPE, H. Displaced subdivision surfaces. In *ACM SIGGRAPH Papers* (New York, NY, USA, 2000), ACM Press, pp. 85–94.

[61] LEYVAND, T., COHEN-OR, D., DROR, G., AND LISCHINSKI, D. Digital face beautification. In *SIGGRAPH '06: ACM SIGGRAPH 2006 Sketches* (New York, NY, USA, 2006), ACM, p. 169.

[62] LORENSEN, W. E., AND CLINE, H. E. Marching cubes: A high resolution 3d surface construction algorithm. In *ACM SIGGRAPH Papers* (New York, NY, USA, 1987), ACM Press, pp. 163–169.

[63] www.MakeHuman.org, 2010.

[64] MARQUARDT, D. W. An algorithm for least-squares estimation of non-linear parameters. *SIAM Journal on Applied Mathematics 11*, 2 (1963), 431–441.

[65] MAYER, R. *Scientific Canadian: Invention and Innovation From Canada's National Research Council.* Raincoast Books, Vancouver, Canada, 1999.

[66] MCDONNELL, R., LARKIN, M., DOBBYN, S., COLLINS, S., AND O'SULLIVAN, C. Clone attack! perception of crowd variety. *ACM Transactions on Graphics 27*, 3 (2008), 1–8.

[67] MELACCI, S., SARTI, L., MAGGINI, M., AND GORI, M. A template-based approach to automatic face enhancement. *Pattern Analysis & Applications* (2009).

[68] MEYER, M., DESBRUN, M., SCHRÖDER, P., AND BARR, A. H. Discrete differential-geometry operators for triangulated 2-manifolds. In *Visualization and Mathematics III* (2003), Springer-Verlag, pp. 35–57.

[69] MITRA, N. J., AND NGUYEN, A. Estimating surface normals in noisy point cloud data. In *SCG '03: Proceedings of the nineteenth annual symposium on Computational geometry* (New York, NY, USA, 2003), ACM, pp. 322–328.

[70] MOESLUND, T., AND GRANUM, E. A survey of computer vision-based human motion capture. *Computer Vision and Image Understanding: CVIU 81*, 3 (2001), 231–268.

[71] MOESLUND, T. B., HILTON, A., AND KRÜGER, V. A survey of advances in vision-based human motion capture and analysis. *Computer Vision and Image Understanding 104*, 2-3 (2006), 90 – 126.

[72] MURRAY, R. M., SASTRY, S. S., AND ZEXIANG, L. *A Mathematical Introduction to Robotic Manipulation*. CRC Press, Inc., Boca Raton, FL, USA, 1994.

[73] MUYBRIDGE, E. *Animal Locomotion*. J. B. Lippincott Co., Philadelphia, PA, USA, 1887.

[74] NOVELLINE, R. A. *Squire's Fundamentals of radiology*. Harvard University Press, 2004.

[75] OGALE, A. S., AND ALOIMONOS, Y. Shape and the stereo correspondence problem. *International Journal of Computer Vision 65*, 3 (2005), 147–162.

[76] PÉREZ, P., GANGNET, M., AND BLAKE, A. Poisson image editing. *ACM Transactions on Graphics 22*, 3 (2003), 313–318.

[77] PINKALL, U., AND POLTHIER, K. Computing discrete minimal surfaces and their conjugates. *Experimental Mathematics 2*, 1 (1993), 15–36.

[78] PLETINCKX, D. Quaternion calculus as a basic tool in computer graphics. *The Visual Computer 5*, 1 (Jan. 1989), 2–13.

[79] REESE, S. *Clay Sculpting for Digital Media*, 1 ed. Prentice Hall, June 2000.

[80] ROBINETTE, K., DAANEN, H., AND PAQUET, E. The caesar project: a 3-d surface anthropometry survey. In *Proc. 3-D Digital Imaging and Modeling* (1999), pp. 380–386.

[81] ROHR, K. Incremental recognition of pedestrians from image sequences. In *IEEE Conference on Computer Vision and Pattern Recognition* (New York, NY, USA, June 1993), pp. 8–13.

[82] ROSENHAHN, B., AND BROX, T. Scaled motion dynamics for markerless motion capture. In *IEEE Conference on Computer Vision and Pattern Recognition* (June 2007), pp. 1–8.

[83] ROSENHAHN, B., SCHMALTZ, C., BROX, T., WEICKERT, J., CREMERS, D., AND SEIDEL, H.-P. Markerless motion capture of man-machine interaction. In *IEEE Conference on Computer Vision and Pattern Recognition* (June 2008), pp. 1–8.

[84] ROTHER, C., KOLMOGOROV, V., AND BLAKE, A. "grabcut": interactive foreground extraction using iterated graph cuts. In *ACM SIGGRAPH Papers* (New York, NY, USA, 2004), ACM Press, pp. 309–314.

[85] SARID, D. Scanning force microscopy. *Oxford Series in Optical and Imaging Sciences* (1991).

[86] SCHAEFER, S., AND YUKSEL, C. Example-based skeleton extraction. In *SGP '07: Proc. Eurographics Symposium on Geometry Processing* (Aire-la-Ville, Switzerland, Switzerland, 2007), Eurographics Association, pp. 153–162.

[87] SCHARSTEIN, D., AND SZELISKI, R. A taxonomy and evaluation of dense two-frame stereo correspondence algorithms. *International Journal of Computer Vision 47*, 1-3 (2002), 7–42.

[88] SCHEEPERS, F., PARENT, R. E., CARLSON, W. E., AND MAY, S. F. Anatomy-based modeling of the human musculature. In *ACM SIGGRAPH Papers* (New York, NY, USA, 1997), ACM Press, pp. 163–172.

[89] SCHENK, T., SEO, S., AND CSATHÓ, B. Accuracy study of airborne laser scanning data with photogrammetry. *International Archives of Photogrammetry and Remote Sensing XXXIV-3/W4* (Oct. 2001), 113–118.

[90] SCHERBAUM, K., SUNKEL, M., SEIDEL, H.-P., AND BLANZ, V. Prediction of individual non-linear aging trajectories of faces. *Eurographics 26*, 3 (2007), 285–294.

[91] SEDERBERG, T. W., AND PARRY, S. R. Free-form deformation of solid geometric models. *SIGGRAPH Comput. Graph. 20*, 4 (1986), 151–160.

[92] SEITZ, S. M., CURLESS, B., DIEBEL, J., SCHARSTEIN, D., AND SZELISKI, R. A comparison and evaluation of multi-view stereo reconstruction algorithms. In *IEEE Conference on Computer Vision and Pattern Recognition* (Washington, DC, USA, 2006), IEEE Computer Society, pp. 519–528.

[93] SEO, H., AND MAGNENAT-THALMANN, N. An example-based approach to human body manipulation. *Graphical Models 66*, 1 (January 2004), 1–23.

[94] SHEFFER, A., AND KRAEVOY, V. Pyramid coordinates for morphing and deformation. In *3DPVT '04: Proceedings of the 3D Data Processing,*

Visualization, and Transmission, 2nd International Symposium (Washington, DC, USA, 2004), IEEE Computer Society, pp. 68–75.

[95] SHI, J., AND TOMASI, C. Good features to track. *IEEE Conference on Computer Vision and Pattern Recognition* (June 1994), 593–600.

[96] SIGAL, L., AND BLACK, M. J. Humaneva: Synchronized video and motion capture dataset for evaluation of articulated human motion. Tech. rep., Brown University, 2006.

[97] SIGAL, L., BĂLAN, A., AND BLACK, M. J. Combined discriminative and generative articulated pose and non-rigid shape estimation. In *NIPS* (2007).

[98] SNAVELY, N., SEITZ, S. M., AND SZELISKI, R. Photo tourism: exploring photo collections in 3d. In *ACM SIGGRAPH Papers* (New York, NY, USA, 2006), ACM Press, pp. 835–846.

[99] SORKINE, O. Laplacian mesh processing. In *Proc. Eurographics - STAR Volume* (2005), Eurographics Association, pp. 53–70.

[100] SORKINE, O. Differential representations for mesh processing. *Computer Graphics Forum 25*, 4 (2006), 789–807.

[101] SORKINE, O., AND ALEXA, M. As-rigid-as-possible surface modeling. In *Proc. symposium on Geometry processing* (Aire-la-Ville, Switzerland, Switzerland, 2007), Eurographics Association, pp. 109–116.

[102] SORKINE, O., COHEN-OR, D., LIPMAN, Y., ALEXA, M., RÖSSL, C., AND SEIDEL, H.-P. Laplacian surface editing. In *Proc. Symposium on Geometry Processing* (New York, NY, USA, 2004), ACM Press, pp. 175–184.

[103] SUMNER, R. W., SCHMID, J., AND PAULY, M. Embedded deformation for shape manipulation. In *ACM SIGGRAPH Papers* (New York, NY, USA, 2007), ACM, p. 80.

[104] SUMNER, R. W., ZWICKER, M., GOTSMAN, C., AND POPOVIĆ, J. Mesh-based inverse kinematics. *ACM Transactions on Graphics 24*, 3 (2005), 488–495.

[105] SUNKEL, M., ROSENHAHN, B., AND SEIDEL, H.-P. Silhouette based generic model adaptation for marker-less motion capturing. In *Proc. of ICCV's 2nd Workshop on Human Motion* (2007), Springer-Verlag, pp. 119–135.

[106] SZELINSKI, R. *Bayesian Modeling of Uncertainty in Low-Level Vision*. Kluwer Academic, Boston, 1977.

[107] TAUBIN, G. A signal processing approach to fair surface design. In *ACM SIGGRAPH Papers* (New York, NY, USA, 1995), ACM Press, pp. 351–358.

[108] TERZOPOULOS, D., PLATT, J., BARR, A., AND FLEISCHER, K. Elastically deformable models. In *ACM SIGGRAPH Papers* (July 1987), ACM Press, pp. 205–214.

[109] TOMASI, C., AND KANADE, T. Shape and motion from image streams under orthography: A factorization method. *International Journal of Computer Vision 9*, 2 (Nov. 1992), 137–154.

[110] VÁRADY, T., MARTIN, R. R., AND COX, J. Reverse engineering of geometric models. *An Introduction, ComputerAided Design 29* (1997), 255–268.

[111] VLASIC, D., BARAN, I., MATUSIK, W., AND POPOVIĆ, J. Articulated mesh animation from multi-view silhouettes. *ACM Transactions on Graphics 27*, 3 (2008), 1–9.

[112] WANG, R. Y., PULLI, K., AND POPOVIĆ, J. Real-time enveloping with rotational regression. In *ACM SIGGRAPH Papers* (New York, NY, USA, 2007), ACM Press, p. 73.

[113] WEBER, O., SORKINE, O., LIPMAN, Y., AND GOTSMAN, C. Context-aware skeletal shape deformation. *Computer Graphics Forum 26*, 3 (Sept. 2007), 265–274.

[114] WREN, C. R., AZARBAYEJANI, A., DARRELL, T., AND PENTLAND, A. P. Pfinder: Real-time tracking of the human body. *IEEE Trans. Pattern Analysis and Machine Intelligence 19*, 7 (July 1997), 780–785.

[115] XU, W., WANG, J., YIN, K., ZHOU, K., VAN DE PANNE, M., CHEN, F., AND GUO, B. Joint-aware manipulation of deformable models. In *SIGGRAPH '09: ACM SIGGRAPH 2009 papers* (New York, NY, USA, 2009), ACM, pp. 1–9.

[116] YU, Y., ZHOU, K., XU, D., SHI, X., BAO, H., GUO, B., AND SHUM, H.-Y. Mesh editing with poisson-based gradient field manipulation. In *ACM SIGGRAPH Papers* (New York, NY, USA, 2004), ACM Press, pp. 644–651.

[117] ZAYER, R., RÖSSL, C., KARNI, Z., AND SEIDEL, H.-P. Harmonic guidance for surface deformation. In *Eurographics* (Dublin, Ireland, 2005), vol. 24 of *Computer Graphics Forum*, Eurographics, Blackwell, pp. 601–609.

[118] ZELNIK-MANOR, L., AND PERONA, P. Self-tuning spectral clustering. In *Advances in Neural Information Processing Systems 17*, L. K. Saul, Y. Weiss, and L. Bottou, Eds. MIT Press, Cambridge, MA, 2005, pp. 1601–1608.

[119] ZHANG, Y. User's guide for yall1: Your algorithms for l1 optimization. Tech. Rep. TR09-17, Rice University, May 2009.

I want morebooks!

Buy your books fast and straightforward online - at one of the world's fastest growing online book stores! Environmentally sound due to Print-on-Demand technologies.

Buy your books online at
www.get-morebooks.com

Kaufen Sie Ihre Bücher schnell und unkompliziert online – auf einer der am schnellsten wachsenden Buchhandelsplattformen weltweit!
Dank Print-On-Demand umwelt- und ressourcenschonend produziert.

Bücher schneller online kaufen
www.morebooks.de

OmniScriptum Marketing DEU GmbH
Heinrich-Böcking-Str. 6-8
D - 66121 Saarbrücken
Telefax: +49 681 93 81 567-9

info@omniscriptum.com
www.omniscriptum.com

Printed by Books on Demand GmbH, Norderstedt / Germany